D0507644

Teach Yourself
VISUALLY™
Mac OS® X Leopard

Visual™

by Lynette Kent

BICENTENNIAL
1807
WILEY
2007
BICENTENNIAL

LAS VEGAS - CLARK COUNTY
LIBRARY DISTRICT
833 LAS VEGAS BLVD, N.
LAS VEGAS, NEVADA 89101

Teach Yourself VISUALLY™ Mac OS® X Leopard

Published by
Wiley Publishing, Inc.
111 River Street
Hoboken, NJ 07030-5774

Published simultaneously in Canada

Copyright © 2007 by Wiley Publishing, Inc., Indianapolis, Indiana

No part of this publication may be reproduced, stored in a retrieval system or transmitted in any form or by any means, electronic, mechanical, photocopying, recording, scanning or otherwise, except as permitted under Sections 107 or 108 of the 1976 United States Copyright Act, without either the prior written permission of the Publisher, or authorization through payment of the appropriate per-copy fee to the Copyright Clearance Center, 222 Rosewood Drive, Danvers, MA 01923, (978) 750-8400, fax (978) 646-8600. Requests to the Publisher for permission should be addressed to the Legal Department, Wiley Publishing, Inc., 10475 Crosspoint Blvd., Indianapolis, IN 46256, (317) 572-3447, fax (317) 572-4355, or online at http://www.wiley.com/go/permissions.

Library of Congress Control Number: 2006939446

ISBN: 978-0-470-10167-4

Manufactured in the United States of America

10 9 8 7 6 5 4 3 2

Trademark Acknowledgments

Wiley, the Wiley Publishing logo, Visual, the Visual logo, Simplified, Master VISUALLY, Teach Yourself VISUALLY, Visual Blueprint, Read Less - Learn More and related trade dress are trademarks or registered trademarks of John Wiley & Sons, Inc. and/or its affiliates. Mac OS is a registered trademark of Apple Inc., and Leopard is a trademark of Apple Inc. All other trademarks are the property of their respective owners. Wiley Publishing, Inc. is not associated with any product or vendor mentioned in this book. *Teach Yourself VISUALLY Mac OS X Leopard* is an independent publication and has not been authorized, sponsored, or otherwise approved by Apple Inc.

LIMIT OF LIABILITY/DISCLAIMER OF WARRANTY: THE PUBLISHER AND THE AUTHOR MAKE NO REPRESENTATIONS OR WARRANTIES WITH RESPECT TO THE ACCURACY OR COMPLETENESS OF THE CONTENTS OF THIS WORK AND SPECIFICALLY DISCLAIM ALL WARRANTIES, INCLUDING WITHOUT LIMITATION WARRANTIES OF FITNESS FOR A PARTICULAR PURPOSE. NO WARRANTY MAY BE CREATED OR EXTENDED BY SALES OR PROMOTIONAL MATERIALS. THE ADVICE AND STRATEGIES CONTAINED HEREIN MAY NOT BE SUITABLE FOR EVERY SITUATION. THIS WORK IS SOLD WITH THE UNDERSTANDING THAT THE PUBLISHER IS NOT ENGAGED IN RENDERING LEGAL, ACCOUNTING, OR OTHER PROFESSIONAL SERVICES. IF PROFESSIONAL ASSISTANCE IS REQUIRED, THE SERVICES OF A COMPETENT PROFESSIONAL PERSON SHOULD BE SOUGHT. NEITHER THE PUBLISHER NOR THE AUTHOR SHALL BE LIABLE FOR DAMAGES ARISING HEREFROM. THE FACT THAT AN ORGANIZATION OR WEBSITE IS REFERRED TO IN THIS WORK AS A CITATION AND/OR A POTENTIAL SOURCE OF FURTHER INFORMATION DOES NOT MEAN THAT THE AUTHOR OR THE PUBLISHER ENDORSES THE INFORMATION THE ORGANIZATION OR WEBSITE MAY PROVIDE OR RECOMMENDATIONS IT MAY MAKE. FURTHER, READERS SHOULD BE AWARE THAT INTERNET WEBSITES LISTED IN THIS WORK MAY HAVE CHANGED OR DISAPPEARED BETWEEN WHEN THIS WORK WAS WRITTEN AND WHEN IT IS READ.

FOR PURPOSES OF ILLUSTRATING THE CONCEPTS AND TECHNIQUES DESCRIBED IN THIS BOOK, THE AUTHOR HAS CREATED VARIOUS NAMES, COMPANY NAMES, MAILING, E-MAIL AND INTERNET ADDRESSES, PHONE AND FAX NUMBERS AND SIMILAR INFORMATION, ALL OF WHICH ARE FICTITIOUS. ANY RESEMBLANCE OF THESE FICTITIOUS NAMES, ADDRESSES, PHONE AND FAX NUMBERS AND SIMILAR INFORMATION TO ANY ACTUAL PERSON, COMPANY AND/OR ORGANIZATION IS UNINTENTIONAL AND PURELY COINCIDENTAL.

Contact Us

For general information on our other products and services please contact our Customer Care Department within the U.S. at 800-762-2974, outside the U.S. at 317-572-3993, or fax 317-572-4002.

For technical support please visit www.wiley.com/techsupport.

Wiley Publishing, Inc.

Sales

Contact Wiley
at (800) 762-2974 or
fax (317) 572-4002.

Praise for Visual Books

"Like a lot of other people, I understand things best when I see them visually. Your books really make learning easy and life more fun."

John T. Frey (Cadillac, MI)

"I have quite a few of your Visual books and have been very pleased with all of them. I love the way the lessons are presented!"

Mary Jane Newman (Yorba Linda, CA)

"I just purchased my third Visual book (my first two are dog-eared now!), and, once again, your product has surpassed my expectations.

Tracey Moore (Memphis, TN)

"I am an avid fan of your Visual books. If I need to learn anything, I just buy one of your books and learn the topic in no time. Wonders! I have even trained my friends to give me Visual books as gifts."

Illona Bergstrom (Aventura, FL)

"Thank you for making it so clear. I appreciate it. I will buy many more Visual books."

J.P. Sangdong (North York, Ontario, Canada)

"I have several books from the Visual series and have always found them to be valuable resources."

Stephen P. Miller (Ballston Spa, NY)

"Thank you for the wonderful books you produce. It wasn't until I was an adult that I discovered how I learn – visually. Nothing compares to Visual books. I love the simple layout. I can just grab a book and use it at my computer, lesson by lesson. And I understand the material! You really know the way I think and learn. Thanks so much!"

Stacey Han (Avondale, AZ)

"I absolutely admire your company's work. Your books are terrific. The format is perfect, especially for visual learners like me. Keep them coming!"

Frederick A. Taylor, Jr. (New Port Richey, FL)

"I have several of your Visual books and they are the best I have ever used."

Stanley Clark (Crawfordville, FL)

"I bought my first Teach Yourself VISUALLY book last month. Wow. Now I want to learn everything in this easy format!"

Tom Vial (New York, NY)

"Thank you, thank you, thank you...for making it so easy for me to break into this high-tech world. I now own four of your books. I recommend them to anyone who is a beginner like myself."

Gay O'Donnell (Calgary, Alberta, Canada)

"I write to extend my thanks and appreciation for your books. They are clear, easy to follow, and straight to the point. Keep up the good work! I bought several of your books and they are just right! No regrets! I will always buy your books because they are the best."

Seward Kollie (Dakar, Senegal)

"Compliments to the chef!! Your books are extraordinary! Or, simply put, extra-ordinary, meaning way above the rest! THANK YOU THANK YOU THANK YOU! I buy them for friends, family, and colleagues."

Christine J. Manfrin (Castle Rock, CO)

"What fantastic teaching books you have produced! Congratulations to you and your staff. You deserve the Nobel Prize in Education in the Software category. Thanks for helping me understand computers."

Bruno Tonon (Melbourne, Australia)

"Over time, I have bought a number of your 'Read Less - Learn More' books. For me, they are THE way to learn anything easily. I learn easiest using your method of teaching."

José A. Mazón (Cuba, NY)

"I am an avid purchaser and reader of the Visual series, and they are the greatest computer books I've seen. The Visual books are perfect for people like myself who enjoy the computer, but want to know how to use it more efficiently. Your books have definitely given me a greater understanding of my computer, and have taught me to use it more effectively. Thank you very much for the hard work, effort, and dedication that you put into this series."

Alex Diaz (Las Vegas, NV)

Credits

Project Editor
Dana Rhodes Lesh

Sr. Acquisitions Editor
Jody Lefevere

Copy Editor
Dana Rhodes Lesh

Technical Editor
Dennis R. Cohen

Editorial Manager
Robyn Siesky

Business Manager
Amy Knies

Sr. Marketing Manager
Sandy Smith

Wiley Bicentennial Logo
Richard J. Pacifico

Manufacturing
Allan Conley
Linda Cook
Paul Gilchrist
Jennifer Guynn

Book Design
Kathie Rickard

Production Coordinator
Adrienne L. Martinez

Layout
Carrie A. Cesavice
Joyce Haughey
Jennifer Mayberry
Amanda Spagnuolo

Screen Artist
Jill A. Proll

Illustrators
Ronda David-Burroughs
Cheryl Grubbs
Shane Johnson

Proofreader
Melissa D. Buddendeck

Quality Control
Laura Albert
David Faust
Susan Moritz

Indexer
Joan K. Griffitts

Vice President and Executive Group Publisher
Richard Swadley

Vice President and Publisher
Barry Pruett

Composition Director
Debbie Stailey

About the Author

Lynette Kent (Huntington Beach, CA) studied art and French at Stanford University. After completing her master's degree, she taught at both the high school and community college level. A fervent Mac user since 1987 and unconventional computer person, she writes books and magazine articles on digital imaging and photography and enjoys presenting computer graphics hardware and software at trade shows. Her books include *Photoshop CS3: Top 100 Simplified Tips & Tricks, Teach Yourself VISUALLY Digital Photography,* and *Scrapbooking with Photoshop Elements: The Creative Cropping Cookbook.* Lynette is also one of the leaders of the Adobe Technology Exchange of Southern California, a professional organization for graphic designers, photographers, and artists.

Author's Acknowledgments

Special thanks go out to acquisitions editor Jody Lefevere for enticing me to write this book; to project editor and copy editor Dana Lesh for her meticulous unscrambling of chapters and for making sure that the text is legible; and to tech editor Dennis Cohen for overseeing the accuracy of the sometimes confusing or complicated steps and guiding my untechnical vocabulary on a technical topic.

Table of Contents

chapter 3 Mastering the Finder

chapter 4 Customizing Leopard

Table of Contents

chapter 5 Using Leopard Applications for Everyday Tasks

chapter 6 Harnessing the Power of the Internet

Table of Contents

chapter 7   Connecting Peripherals to Your Mac

chapter 8   Listening to Music, Radio, and Podcasts

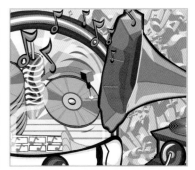

Table of Contents

chapter 12 Troubleshooting Mac Problems

DE-ICER
Force Quit
without
Rebooting
Your
Computer

How to Use This Book

How to Use This *Teach Yourself VISUALLY* Book

Do you look at the pictures in a book or newspaper before anything else on a page? Would you rather see an image instead of read about how to do something? Search no further. This book is for you. Opening *Teach Yourself VISUALLY Mac OS X Leopard* enables you to read less and learn more about the new 10.5 Mac operating system.

Who Needs This Book

This book is for a reader who has never used this particular technology or software application. It is also for more computer-literate individuals who want to expand their knowledge of the different features that Mac OS X Leopard has to offer.

Book Organization

Teach Yourself VISUALLY Mac OS X Leopard has 12 chapters:

Chapter 1, "Getting Started with Mac OS X Leopard Fundamentals," covers using the mouse, installing and setting up Leopard, and general Macintosh basics.

Chapter 2, "Working with Separate Applications," discusses techniques for using all types of applications with Leopard.

In Chapter 3, "Mastering the Finder," I explain how to use the basic Mac interface and where things are located.

Chapter 4, "Customizing Leopard," covers setting up your system to suit your work.

Chapter 5, "Using Leopard Applications for Everyday Tasks," goes over the included productivity applications and how to use them.

Chapter 6, "Harnessing the Power of the Internet," explains how to use Apple's Safari Web browser and Apple's email application, called *Mail*.

In Chapter 7, "Connecting Peripherals to Your Mac," you learn about techniques for using external hardware attached to your Mac.

Chapter 8, "Listening to Music, Radio, and Podcasts," discusses the various audio-related applications included with Leopard.

Chapter 9, "Working with Images and Video," covers the various image-related applications included with Leopard.

Chapter 10, "Connecting to Other Machines over a Network," offers various tips and techniques for setting up networks to share files and chats.

Chapter 11, "Simplifying Tasks and Maintenance," gives you simple tips and techniques for regular maintenance and avoiding problems.

In Chapter 12, "Troubleshooting Mac Problems," you find out about techniques for resolving software problems if they do occur.

Chapter Organization

This book consists of sections, all listed in the book's table of contents. A *section* is a set of steps that shows you how to complete a specific computer task.

Each section, usually contained on two facing pages, has an introduction to the task at hand, a set of full-color screenshots and steps that walk you through the task, and a set of tips. This format enables you to quickly look at a topic of interest and learn it instantly.

Chapters group together six or more sections with a common theme. A chapter may also contain pages that give you the background information needed to understand the sections in the chapter.

What You Need to Use This Book

You need to have a newer Macintosh computer with System 10.5 loaded, or you need the Mac OS 10.5 (Leopard) install DVD and a Mac capable of running Mac OS X Leopard, including an Intel iMac, a Mac Pro, a MacBook, a MacBook Pro, or a newer PowerPC Macintosh with built-in FireWire. You will also need at least 256MB of RAM for a PowerPC-based Mac and 512MB for an Intel-based Mac. Additional RAM is highly recommended, a built-in display or a display connected to an Apple-supplied video card supported by your computer, and at least 6GB of disk space available just to install the system.

Using the Mouse

This book uses the following conventions to describe the actions you perform when using the mouse:

Click

Press the mouse button once. You generally click your mouse on something to select something on the screen.

Double-click

Press the mouse button twice quickly. Double-clicking something on the computer screen generally opens whatever item you have double-clicked.

Click and Drag and Release the Mouse Button

Move your mouse pointer and hover it over an item on the screen. Press and hold down the mouse button. Now, move the mouse to where you want to place the item and then release the button. You use this method to move an item from one area of the computer screen to another.

The Conventions in This Book

A number of typographic and layout styles have been used throughout *Teach Yourself VISUALLY Mac OS X Leopard* to distinguish different types of information.

Bold

Bold type represents the names of commands and options that you interact with. Bold type also indicates text and numbers that you must type into a dialog box or window.

Italics

Italic words introduce a new term and are followed by a definition.

Numbered Steps

You must perform the instructions in numbered steps in order to successfully complete a section and achieve the final results.

Bulleted Steps

These steps point out various optional features. You do not have to perform these steps; they simply give additional information about a feature.

Indented Text

Indented text tells you what the program does in response to you following a numbered step. For example, if you click a certain menu command, a dialog box may appear, or a window may open. Indented text may also tell you what the final result is when you follow a set of numbered steps.

Notes

Notes give additional information. They may describe special conditions that may occur during an operation. They may warn you of a situation that you want to avoid — for example, the loss of data. A note may also cross-reference a related area of the book. A cross-reference may guide you to another chapter or another section within the current chapter.

Icons and Buttons

Icons and buttons are graphical representations within the text. They show you exactly what you need to click to perform a step.

 You can easily identify the tips in any section by looking for the TIPS icon. Tips offer additional information, including tips, hints, and tricks. You can use the TIPS information to go beyond what you have learned in the steps.

CHAPTER 1

Getting Started with Mac OS X Leopard Fundamentals

Mac OS X Leopard, also known as Mac OS 10.5, is Apple's latest operating system. The Mac OS is the underlying software that runs your Macintosh computer and enables you to interact with the computer using a mouse and a keyboard. Leopard includes a variety of built-in programs to help you work or play and even get entertainment on your Mac.

The Macintosh Operating System, abbreviated *OS*, is actually the most important program running on a Macintosh. Leopard is version 10.5 of Apple's most advanced operating system to date. Understanding Leopard and familiarizing yourself with some Leopard tricks make everything you do with your computer much faster and more fun.

The Central Command Post

The operating system controls all the hardware and software connected to or installed on your computer. It controls the input from devices such as the mouse and keyboard and the output to the monitor and printer. The OS keeps track of all your files and folders on your computer, as well as any additional data on external disk drives.

Leopard and Computer Hardware

The Mac OS is responsible for understanding and acting on the information that you send to it by pressing keys on the keyboard, clicking the mouse, or using the trackpad. Mac OS X Leopard enables you to personalize the feel of your mouse and keyboard as well as the screen display using the many options in System Preferences.

Run Applications

The Mac OS enables your computer to run application software so that you can accomplish a variety of tasks and projects better and more quickly than using a traditional pen and paper and other noncomputer methods.

Surf the Internet and Send Email

Leopard provides you with everything that you need to surf the World Wide Web. The included Safari Web browser gives you the means to view Web pages. Leopard's Mail program gives you access to the world of email.

Share Files and Hardware with Others

The Mac OS helps you connect to other computers anywhere on a local network, whether wired or wireless. You can share files as well as hardware such as printers with others on the network.

Interface with Other Equipment

The Mac OS helps you connect and work with a variety of external hardware, such as different types of mice, keyboards, scanners and other input devices, and external disk drives, as well as iPods, cameras, cell phones, and printers.

Before you install Leopard on your Mac, you must check the hardware requirements of the new operating system. Your third-party applications may need to be upgraded so that they will function with Leopard. In addition, your hard disk must have sufficient space available and be checked for disk errors. The type of installation that you select depends on your current system.

Check the Hardware Requirements

You can install Leopard on newer Macintosh computers with a DVD drive and built-in FireWire, including PowerPC G4s and G5s and Intel Macintoshes. Although the standard installation of Leopard requires about 11GB of free hard drive space and 512MB RAM, having at least 20GB of available hard drive space and 1GB or more of RAM will enhance your computer's performance.

Check Your Favorite Software

Third-party software manufacturers work with the operating system during its development so that they can update their applications in time for a new Mac OS release. If you need a specific application, you should check with the manufacturer to see if it will work with Mac OS X Leopard.

Back Up Your Hard Drive

If possible, make a bootable backup of your current system on an external drive using an application such as Personal Backup X4 from www.intego.com or Carbon Copy Cloner from www.bombich.com. You can start up from this drive to finish projects or reinstall the old system if you encounter problems after upgrading.

Check Your Disk for Errors

Insert the Leopard DVD. Click the Install Mac OS X icon to restart from the DVD. Type your administrator password in the dialog box, select your preferred language in the first window, and click the forward arrow. When the Install window appears, click **Utilities** in the menu. Click **Disk Utility** and check your hard drive as described in Chapter 12. Click the Close button (⊙) to quit Disk Utility.

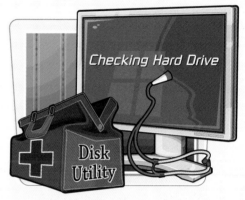

Select an Installation Type

Continue the installation. Click a hard drive in the Select a Destination panel and click **Options** to select an installation type. **Upgrade Mac OS X** simply updates the system software. To install a new copy of Mac OS X while keeping your existing user accounts and settings, click **Archive and Install** and **Preserve Users and Network Settings**. Clicking **Erase and Install** completely erases all data on the destination volume and installs a pristine system similar to that on a new computer.

Use the Time Machine

When you continue, a Time Machine option appears. If you have an external drive attached, click **Back up my disk before installing**. Time Machine creates an additional backup of your existing system. Continue with the installation, which can take some time.

Whether you just bought a new Mac and are starting it up for the first time or you have installed Mac OS X Leopard on a Mac with a previous operating system, you have a number of options for setting up and personalizing your Macintosh and Leopard.

The Leopard Welcome Screen

Like all Mac operating systems, Leopard welcomes you in multiple languages. A Mac OS X box spins around, asking various questions to guide you through the installation process, starting with the country or region where you are located.

Transferring Information

Previous Mac users can automatically transfer data from another Mac attached with a FireWire cable. You can also transfer from another volume, meaning previous files on the same computer. You can also transfer the information later by choosing not to transfer any data. The built-in software assistant enables you to migrate the information later.

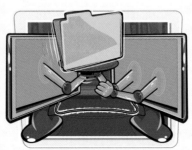

Your Apple ID

If your computer is connected to the Internet, you can create an Apple ID and password during the installation. Your Apple ID is a free personalized information account that you can use with future Apple online and iTunes purchases, as well as AppleCare support.

A .Mac Account

The free .Mac (pronounced *dot mac*) account is used for activities such as iChat. A paid .Mac membership includes email and personalized iDisk storage space online and is useful for publishing Web sites and syncing your Address Book and iCal calendars with multiple computers.

Create a Leopard User Account

The first time that you start a new operating system, you create a user account. The main user account controls the software that can be installed and limits others who use the same computer. Other accounts can be created later.

Select a Picture

Each user account can have an icon identifier. You can choose one of Leopard's included icons, or if your Mac has an iSight camera, you can take a snapshot of yourself to use with your account. The icon can be changed at any time.

New Backup Option for Installing Leopard

If you are installing Mac OS X Leopard on a computer with a previous Mac operating system, you can back up your existing system and files before you install, as mentioned earlier. Time Machine automatically creates a searchable backup and stores it on a separate volume on your main hard drive if you have partitioned the drive, or preferably on an external drive, as discussed in Chapter 11.

Click, Double-Click, or Click and Drag

You can open and close documents, move items from one place to another on your screen, and control how your computer works all by clicking, double-clicking, or clicking and dragging the mouse or trackpad.

Click, Double-Click, or Click and Drag

CLICK

1 Click the Finder button (🗂) in the Dock.

A Finder window opens if one is not already open.

2 Click a folder to select it.

3 Click **File**.

4 Click **Open**.

The folder opens, revealing its contents.

DOUBLE-CLICK

① In the Finder, double-click a folder icon.

The folder opens immediately.

Note: Double-click a file within a folder to open that file and the application that created it.

CLICK AND DRAG

① In the Finder, click and drag a folder out of the Finder window.

② Release the mouse button.

The file appears outside the Finder window on the desktop.

 TIPS

Can I rename a folder with one click?

You can rename a file or folder by clicking its name in the Finder. Press Return, and the name appears highlighted. Type the name and press Return to complete the change.

What shortcuts will help me?

Press Control as you click any icon once and a contextual menu opens, revealing different options. Press ⌘ as you double-click a folder, and the folder opens in a new window. Press Option as you double-click a folder to open it in a separate window while closing the previous window.

Understanding the Mac Interface

Although Xerox Corporation's research center originally designed a mouse-driven graphical user interface (GUI), Apple created the first computer to popularize a GUI, freeing the user from learning complex commands. The Apple Mac interface uses icons grouped on a desktop, along with windows and a menu system. Getting familiar with the interface is the key to working efficiently and having fun with the Mac.

Your View of the Monitor Screen

When Leopard first opens, your screen displays a green grass background that you can change, a top menu bar, the Dock with icons at the bottom, a hard drive icon in the top-right corner, and a cursor.

Icons

Icons are central to the Mac OS interface. Clicking an icon selects it, and double-clicking it opens the file and launches the associated application. You can click and drag icons to different locations to customize your workspace.

The Dock

The Dock is a convenient way to launch applications, quickly access downloaded files, or open often-used files and folders from a stack. You can move, remove, and add other application and file icons to the Dock and even customize its size and location on the screen.

The Menu Bar

The horizontal menu at the top offers numerous options hidden under each word or icon on it. Click a word to reveal a drop-down menu of actions for your task.

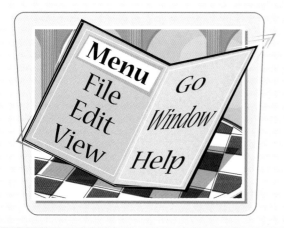

Work from the Desktop

The desktop is a metaphor used to describe the top level of the filing system. It is the background area of your screen where you can access and organize your hard drive and all your files, icons, and windows.

Find It in the Finder

The Finder is a software program that is always running. It is basically a file-management system for all the components of the interface. The Finder helps you work with files, desktop icons, and windows, as well as other disks.

Applications

Leopard includes a variety of applications and helps you install other Apple and third-party applications for writing text, creating spreadsheets, listening to and creating music, and viewing and creating videos, photos, and other graphics.

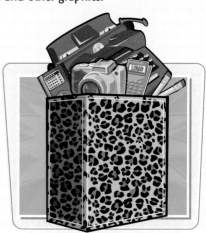

Control the Mac with Menus

You can open items, make selections, and start other applications using the menu bar. The menu choices sometimes vary depending on the application; however, the overall look and many of the options remain the same. You can also use keyboard shortcuts to access some menu items, and the shortcuts are most often the same across various applications.

Control the Mac with Menus

CLICK A MENU

①   In the Finder, click the command with the options that you want to open, such as **Go**.

A menu drops down with more options.

②   Click the option that you want, such as **Home**.

In this example, a window opens, showing the contents of your Home folder.

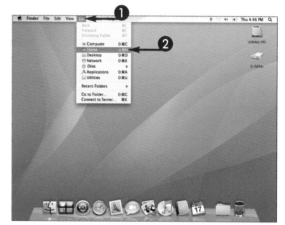

USE A KEYBOARD SHORTCUT TO SELECT MENU ITEMS

1 Click the background area of the desktop.

2 Press the keyboard shortcut for the option that you want, such as ⌘ + Shift + U for the Utilities folder.

A window opens, listing the contents of the Utilities folder.

 TIPS

What are the small icons on the far-right side of the menu bar?

The menu bar actually has three parts. The Apple icon on the far left is always the same. The name of the open application, such as "Finder," is bolded with its specific menu options next to it. The icons on the right are status menus and shortcuts to certain features such as the sound volume or date and time.

Are there any keys that produce hidden functions in the menus?

You can press Option and Shift to reveal hidden menu functions. Hidden menu items appear in place of the usual menu items when you press these modifier keys. For example, in the Finder menu, click File and press Option. The Get Info selection changes to Show Inspector.

Open, Close, and Resize Windows on the Desktop

Windows are an integral part of the Mac OS interface. The Finder and many applications have windows. You can open, close, move, and even hide or minimize windows with the click of a mouse. You can also change the size of a window by clicking and dragging.

Open, Close, and Resize Windows on the Desktop

OPEN A NEW WINDOW

1 In the Finder, click **File**.

2 Click **New Finder Window**.

The Finder window opens.

Note: The Finder window is the same as your Home folder window by default, but you can change this in the Finder Preferences.

RESIZE AND MOVE A FINDER WINDOW

1 Click and drag the bottom-right corner of the window.

The window resizes as you drag.

2 Click the green Zoom button (◎).

The window zooms to full size.

3 Click ◎ again.

The window returns to its original size.

4 Click and drag the title bar of the window.

The window moves around on the screen.

CLOSE A FINDER WINDOW

① Click the red Close button ().

The window closes.

Note: *Closing a window may or may not quit the application, depending on which application is running.*

MINIMIZE A FINDER WINDOW

① Click the yellow Minimize button ().

The window shrinks down to fit as an icon in the Dock.

② Click the window icon on the right side of the Dock.

The window returns to the desktop at its original size.

TIPS

Can I use the keyboard to control the sizing of windows?

Yes. You can press ⌘+M to minimize the foremost window and shrink it to the Dock. Pressing ⌘+W closes the foremost window. If you press Option when you click 🔴, all the open windows of the same application close at once. You can press ⌘+Option+W to close all the open windows at once using only the keyboard.

Are there other keyboard shortcuts for windows?

Yes. You can cycle through all the open windows of one application by repeatedly pressing ⌘+~. You can keep pressing ⌘+Shift+~ to cycle through the windows in reverse order.

Change Your View

As with most features of the Mac OS, you can personalize the way items appear on your desktop. You can resize items to fit your monitor and your vision, arrange them in different ways or force them to line up on a grid, and more. Keeping the desktop arranged helps you find and open items much more easily.

Change Your View

① With no windows open on the desktop, click **View**.

② Click **Show View Options**.

A dialog box for the desktop view options appears.

③ Click and drag the Icon Size ⬚.

All the icons on the desktop change size.

④ Click and drag the Grid Spacing ⬚.

The hard drive icon moves closer or farther from the edge of the screen.

Note: *If you have multiple icons on the desktop, the changes will affect all of them at once.*

5 Click the Text Size ⬍.

6 Select a new text size.

The size of the text under the hard drive icon changes.

7 Click **Right** (◯ changes to ◉).

The icon text now aligns to the right of the hard drive icon.

8 Click **Show item info** (☐ changes to ☑).

The number of items or the size of the drive is added to the name.

Note: Clicking **Show icon preview** only changes the look of the icon if its contents are a graphic, such as a photo.

9 Click the Arrange By ⬍.

10 Click **Name**.

The icons on the desktop all line up evenly spaced.

Note: The other selections on the Arrange By menu arrange the icons with different specifications.

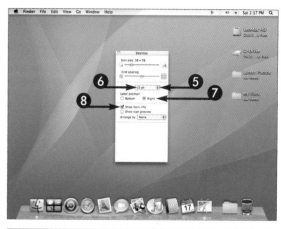

TIPS

What does Snap to Grid do?

When you click **Snap to Grid** on the Arrange By pop-up menu, the icons in the window are forced onto a grid, keeping your window neatly arranged. No matter where on the window you drag an icon, it will always snap into an evenly spaced position away from the other icons in the window.

Why does the Macintosh hard drive icon always return to the top, no matter where I try to move it — even when I select a different View option?

The drive icon with the startup system on it always returns to the top-right corner on the desktop. If you have other drives with a Mac OS system on them attached, such as an external hard drive or a DVD in the optical drive, the icon at the top of the list represents the drive that booted or started up the computer.

Create and Name a Folder

The Mac OS uses a hierarchical file system. The concept is the same as the filing system that you would use with a traditional filing cabinet. You can create and name a folder to contain all the files for one project. You can also create and name multiple folders within another folder to further categorize your projects and files.

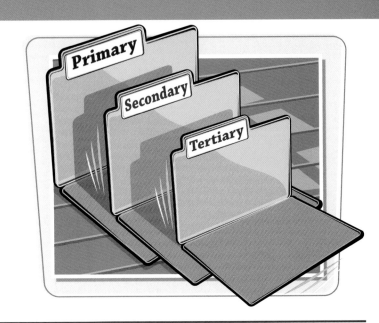

Create and Name a Folder

① In a Finder window, click **File**.

② Click **New Folder**.

A folder icon labeled "untitled folder" appears in the window.

③ Type a name for the new folder before pressing any other keys.

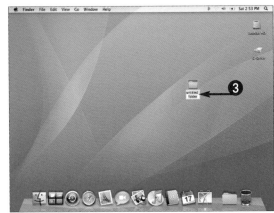

• The new name appears in an editable box under the folder.

4 Press Return.

The name is now the name for the folder.

 TIPS

Can I rename older folders the same way as a new one?

Yes. You can rename files, folders, and disks in the Finder or Home folder items. Click the icon and press Return. Type the new name and press Return again. You should not change the name of the Home folder itself, the name of application files and folders, or items that came in the Leopard Mac OS system, such as the Library folder.

Can I use any letters and numbers in a folder name?

Yes. You can create any name and use any letters and numbers. Avoid using symbols in file and folder names because some symbols are specific to certain applications and others are not allowed. Never use a colon in a filename or start a filename with a period. Many applications also reject a forward slash in a filename.

Logging In and Out

Mac OS X Leopard is designed to allow more than one person to use a computer — with each user having his or her own personalized settings and Home folder. When you first set up Leopard, you create an administrator account with a name and password. When you log out, another person can log in with his or her name and password. This way each user's settings and individual files are protected.

Logging In and Out

① Click the Apple icon (🍎).

② Click **Log Out**.

Note: The name of the current user is next to Log Out on the menu.

A window appears asking you to confirm the log out operation.

Note: You can press and hold Option *when clicking Log Out to bypass the confirmation dialog box.*

③ Click **Log Out**.

All running applications and open files are closed, and the screen turns blue.

A new Log In window appears listing all the available users.

④ Click the username that you want if there is more than one.

The Log In window for that user opens.

⑤ Type the password for that user in the data field.

⑥ Click **Log In**.

Note: *You can also press* Return *after typing the password.*

The Finder reopens with the personalized settings for the new user.

 TIPS

How come I do not get a Log In window when I start up my computer?

If you do not see a Log In window at startup, your Account Preferences are set to automatically log in for a specific user. Automatic login is faster and more convenient. If others use your computer, you can change the automatic login settings in your Account Preferences in System Preferences. See Chapter 4 for more information.

What is the advantage of logging out when I am finished working on the computer?

Logging out adds a measure of security. If you log out of your user account when you are finished with the computer, you can leave the computer turned on, yet no one else can see your work or change your settings.

Put Your Mac to Sleep

You can put your computer to sleep instead of shutting it down when you need to stop for a while but want to resume working exactly where you left off. Putting your Mac to sleep is especially useful for laptop computers when using battery power. A sleeping Mac uses less energy while still allowing instant-on access.

Put Your Mac to Sleep

MAKE ANY MAC GO TO SLEEP

1 Click .

2 Click **Sleep**.

The screen turns black, and the Mac goes to sleep.

WAKE YOUR MAC UP

1 Press any key or click the mouse button.

The computer awakens with all the open documents and applications exactly as they were before.

PUT A LAPTOP TO SLEEP QUICKLY

1 Close the laptop lid.

The computer goes to sleep.

Note: *Most laptop Mac models show a pulsating external light to indicate a sleeping computer.*

2 Open the lid and press any key to awaken the laptop.

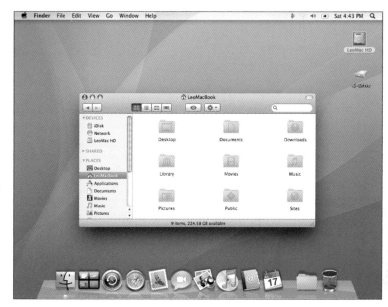

What happens when a Mac is in sleep mode?

When you put a Mac to sleep, it puts the computer in a low-power mode. It will remember unsaved documents that you were working on; however, it is always best to save your work before putting the computer to sleep. The sleep mode also disables the network settings, preventing file sharing on the network.

Do I still have to worry about the battery running out on my laptop while it sleeps?

Yes. Although the computer uses a low-power mode during sleep, it is still using battery power. When a laptop battery gets below a certain level of remaining power, the Mac shuts off automatically, and you could lose any unsaved data.

Restart or
Shut Down the Mac

Installing software applications or updating the system software generally requires the computer to restart. Restarting can also help when a computer is not responding properly.

Although a Mac can run nonstop, you may choose to shut it down at various times. You must shut it down when you move the machine, during an electrical storm, or to install certain new hardware.

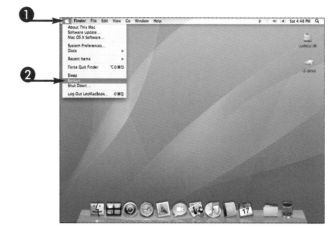

Turn ON

Turn OFF

Restart

Restart or Shut Down the Mac

RESTART A MAC

① Click .

② Click **Restart**.

A dialog box appears, asking you to approve the restart.

Note: *You can press and hold* Option *when clicking* ***Restart*** *to bypass the confirmation dialog box.*

③ Click **Restart**.

The computer restarts.

SHUT DOWN A MAC

1 Click .

2 Click **Shut Down**.

A dialog box asks you to approve the shutdown process.

Note: You can press and hold Option when clicking **Shut Down** to bypass the confirmation dialog box.

3 Click **Shut Down**.

The computer shuts down.

TIPS

What happens when my computer restarts?

When you restart, your computer turns off and immediately turns on again, but never stops the hard drive. Your desktop reappears quickly with all your personal settings. If you use a computer in a multiuser environment, you may have to provide a login username and password when you restart the computer.

What is the difference between restarting and shutting down and then starting up the computer with the power button?

Both restarting and shutting down close all the open applications and documents and disconnect the network and Internet. Restarting is faster than shutting down and starting the computer with the power button. Shutting down turns the computer completely off. When you turn it back on, the computer goes through a number of self-checks before it is ready.

Using the Help Menu

The Mac OS system and most Mac applications include a very useful Help function. Help is located on the menu bar and offers both a search field and a direct link to various options and help documents, depending on the application. You can find answers to many questions about the Mac OS in the Help menu in the Finder.

Using the Help Menu

① In the Finder menu bar, click **Help**.

② Click **Mac Help**.

The Help Viewer launches and displays a Mac Help window.

③ Type a question or topic into the search field.

④ Press Return.

The Help Viewer displays a list of topics related to your question.

⑤ Click a topic to select it.

⑥ Click **Show**.

Note: You can also press `Return` *to show the topic information.*

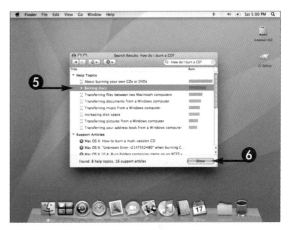

Mac Help displays a detailed answer to the question.

⑦ Click ◄ to go back to the previous window.

Note: You can return to the main Mac Help window at any time by clicking the Home button (⌂ ▼) in the Mac Help window.

 TIPS

How do I locate help for applications other than the Finder and Mac OS?

The menu bar is specific to each open application. When you click Help in one application, the Help Viewer displays information specific to that current application.

Are all the help files located on my computer?

Some help files are stored with the application folder, and others are linked to the Internet. The Help Viewer will list links to documents on your computer as well those on the Internet. You can click links to Web pages that automatically open in Safari or your default Web browser.

CHAPTER 2

Working with Separate Applications

The Mac OS is the brain that runs your computer. It acts as the bottom platform on top of which other programs, called *applications,* can run. Apple includes a number of applications with Leopard and also sells more advanced or involved ones separately. Other manufacturers, both well-known and smaller software developers, also sell a wide variety of useful applications for the Mac OS, and some even offer free applications called *freeware.*

Understanding Applications

Applications are the main workhorses of any type of computer. They help you perform a variety of tasks with a computer to replace traditional methods of working. Without applications, a computer is merely an electronic box that turns on and off and acts as a storage device for files.

Types of Applications

You can write anything from letters to books with word-processing applications and analyze data with spreadsheet applications. Web browsers, such as Safari, connect you with the Internet, and email applications, such as Apple's Mail, enable you to read and write email. You can edit images and video, play and create music, or draw and paint with different applications.

Applications and File Types

Files have an extension in the name, such as .doc, .jpg, or .txt, to denote the file type and usually the application that created it. Some applications can create, save, and open only one kind of file. Others create and save one kind of file but can open various file types. Still others can work with a variety of file types.

Mac OS X Leopard's Applications

The Leopard operating system automatically installs a number of applications, including the Time Machine backup, a Web browser, an email application, a calendar, a dictionary, the Spotlight search application, a calculator, a simple text application, iTunes for listening to music, QuickTime for watching videos, and many other fun and useful applications.

Other Applications for Mac OS X Leopard

Apple also makes separate applications and application suites, such as iLife and iWork. These applications are sometimes included when you purchase a new Mac computer. Other manufacturers make a wide variety of applications that you can use with the Mac OS.

About the Applications Folder

The most important folders in the Mac operating system are at the top level of the hierarchical organization. These include the system software itself, individual accounts and settings, and the Applications folder. Most installers automatically install an application in the Applications folder.

Learning to Use Applications

Most applications have basic similarities, including the menu bar and many of the submenus. Many also offer online help found in the Help menu. Others are very complex and often do not include sufficient information in the manual. Educational books such as the *Teach Yourself VISUALLY* series offer the quickest way to learn to use these applications.

Before you can use an application, you need to install it on the system. Installers are included when you purchase an application on CD or DVD or download an application using the Internet. Either way, installing applications on the Mac OS is easy.

Install an Application

1 Insert the CD or DVD.

The disc icon appears on the desktop.

2 Double-click the disc icon to open it.

Note: If you downloaded the software, double-click the downloaded file icon.

The contents of the disc appear in a window.

3 Double-click the application's installer icon.

Note: The application installer icons can vary. Some display the application, and others show a package icon. Some installers specify that you click and drag the application to the desktop or Applications folder for installation.

4 Follow the onscreen instructions.

A dialog box appears, requiring a name and password.

Note: *Many application installers require you to agree to the licensing terms before proceeding.*

⑤ Type your computer name or administrator account name if necessary.

⑥ Type your account password.

⑦ Click **OK**.

The installer proceeds with the installation.

A message window appears saying that the application was successfully installed.

⑧ Click Close.

 TIPS

Where should I install applications?
During the install process, most installers ask you to choose a folder to install the application. The default location is usually the Applications folder on the startup drive. It is generally best to install all your applications in the Applications folder.

I downloaded an application, and there is an icon on my desktop with .dmg at the end. What should I do?
A .dmg file is a disc image. Some downloaded files automatically open to show a folder with an installer icon after downloading. Others require you to open the disc image first. Double-click the disc image icon and then proceed with step **3** and the subsequent steps as shown here.

Start and Quit an Application

You need to launch an application to use it or to work on an existing file created with that application or a similar one. You can start an application directly from the Applications folder by double-clicking its icon. You can quit any running application from that application's menu or use a keyboard shortcut.

Start and Quit an Application

START AN APPLICATION

1 In the Finder menu bar, click **Go**.

2 Click **Applications**.

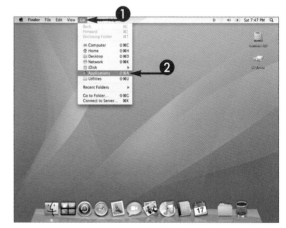

The Applications window opens.

Note: *Finder windows can be viewed four different ways: as icons, as a list, in columns, or in Cover Flow mode as shown here.*

3 Click and drag here to scroll through the icons until the application that you want to launch is visible.

4 Double-click the icon.

● Optionally, you can double-click the name of the application in the list.

The application launches.

● When you launch TextEdit, an untitled document appears on the desktop, as shown in this example.

Note: Some applications open a document, and others open a dialog box asking you what to open.

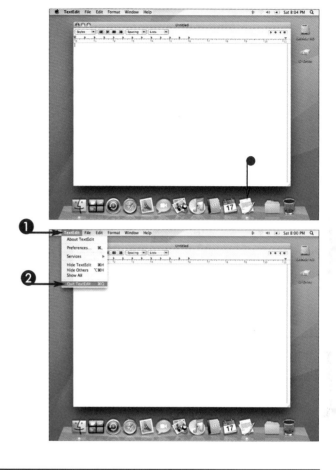

QUIT AN APPLICATION

① In the menu bar, click the application's name.

② Click **Quit *ApplicationName***.

Note: The bolded word on the left in the menu always refers to the currently running application.

Note: In TextEdit, clicking the Close button () on the document window only closes the document; it does not quit the application. Clicking in utility applications does quit the application.

TIPS

Is there a keyboard shortcut to open the Applications folder or to quit an application?

Yes. Click once on the desktop to make sure that you are in the Finder. Press ⌘ + Shift + A. The Applications window opens directly. To quit a running application with a keyboard shortcut, press ⌘ + Q.

Do I always have to start with the Applications folder to start an application?

If you have a file icon on your desktop or visible in any open folder, you can double-click the icon. The application that created the file will start up and open the document at the same time. If the application's icon is in the Dock, or if a file is in a folder or stack in the Dock, you can single-click the icon to launch the application.

Using the Dock to Start and Quit an Application

The Dock on the bottom of your desktop includes a number of application icons. You can click a Dock icon to launch that application; however, you can also launch any application in the Applications folder by first clicking the Finder icon in the Dock. Using the Dock is a quick way to access almost everything on a Mac.

Using the Dock to Start and Quit an Application

START AN APPLICATION FROM THE DOCK

① Click the Finder icon (⛫) in the Dock.

The Finder window representing your Home folder opens.

Note: You can change the Finder Preferences so that a new Finder window opens a different folder.

② Click **Applications** in the sidebar.

The window changes to the Applications window.

③ Click and drag the scrollbars or the Cover Flow bar to see the application that you want to start.

④ Double-click the application's icon.

Note: For certain applications, such as iTunes, the first time that you launch them on your computer, you must agree to the licensing agreement before proceeding.

● The application opens on the desktop, and its icon appears in the Dock.

QUIT AN APPLICATION FROM THE DOCK

① Click and hold the application's icon in the Dock.

② Click **Quit**.

The application closes.

Note: See Chapter 4 to customize the look of the Dock.

Why did a ▨ suddenly appear below an icon in the Dock?

Whenever you launch an application or start one that is already in the Dock, a ▨ denotes that the application is running. When you close an application, the ▨ disappears. The Dock is the easiest way to see what applications are currently running on the Mac.

Why is there always a space in my Dock even when I readjust the size?

The space in the Dock separates any applications from the files and folders that you place in the Dock. Anytime you drag a file or folder to the Dock, it is placed to the right of the space next to the Trash icon.

Add a Favorite Application to the Dock

Keeping your most frequently used applications in the Dock saves you time and many keystrokes. You can add any application to the Dock by simply clicking and dragging its icon onto the Dock. You can also remove the icon from the Dock just as easily.

Add a Favorite Application to the Dock

ADD AN APPLICATION TO THE DOCK

① In the Finder, click **Go**.

② Click **Applications**.

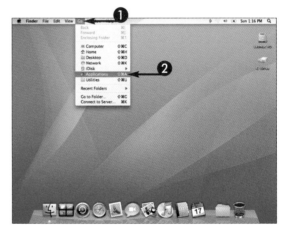

The Applications window opens.

③ Click and drag any of the scrollbars to find the application to add.

④ Click and drag the icon of the application over the Dock.

⑤ Release the mouse button.

The application's icon slips into place in the Dock.

KEEP AN ALREADY RUNNING APPLICATION IN THE DOCK

1 In the Applications window, double-click the application's icon.

Note: If the application is already running, you can skip step 1.

The application appears on the desktop, and its icon appears in the Dock.

2 Click and hold the application's icon in the Dock.

3 Click **Keep in Dock**.

The application's icon will now remain in the Dock, even after you close the application.

REMOVE AN APPLICATION FROM THE DOCK

1 Click and drag the application's icon outside the Dock.

Note: To remove an application from the Dock, you must first quit the application.

The icon disappears in a puff of smoke.

Note: See Chapter 4 for more tricks on customizing the Dock.

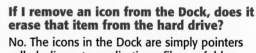

TIPS

Can I add other items to the Dock?

You can add icons for files, folders, Web sites, photos, and more to the Dock to make them quickly accessible. Application icons will always be placed to the left of the space, with files and folders placed in a stack next to the right next to the Trash icon.

If I remove an icon from the Dock, does it erase that item from the hard drive?

No. The icons in the Dock are simply pointers called *aliases* to applications, files, or folders. Removing an icon from the Dock affects only your ability to access it from the Dock. It does not affect the actual application, file, or folder in your system or on your hard drive.

Using a Stack to Access Applications

You can use the new Stacks feature of Leopard to keep all your applications available in the Dock. By creating a stack of the Applications folder, you can quickly access any application by clicking the folder in the Dock and clicking the Application icon to launch it.

Using a Stack to Access Applications

① Double-click the hard drive icon on the desktop.

The hard drive window opens.

② Click and drag the Applications folder to the right side of the Dock, next to the folder by the Trash icon.

③ Release the mouse button.

A folder stack appears in the Dock.

④ Click the Applications stack.

A transparent grid appears of all the icons of the Applications in the folder.

⑤ Click an icon to launch its application.

● The selected application launches, and its icon is added to the Dock to show that it is running.

● The Application stack displays the Applications symbol on the folder.

My Dock already has a folder in it. What does that folder contain?

The folder that appears in the Dock represents a stack for downloaded documents. When you download in the Safari Web browser or save a Mail attachment from an email, the files are by default placed in a Downloads folder inside your Home folder.

I accidentally moved the Downloads stack off the Dock. How can I get it back?

You have only removed the alias from the Dock. You have not lost your Downloads folder. Open a Finder window and click the Home folder. Click and drag the Downloads folder icon onto the Dock just to the left of the Trash icon and release the mouse button. Leopard places a new alias of the folder in the Dock.

Toggle between Running Applications

You can quickly switch to any running application using the Application Switcher. You can launch this hidden utility with a keystroke, and it disappears just as quickly when you release the keys. The Application Switcher is another small built-in utility to help you work on a Mac.

Toggle between Running Applications

① Press and hold ⌘.

② Press Tab once while still pressing ⌘.

The Application Switcher displays all the running applications.

③ Press Tab again.

● The Application Switcher highlights the next icon in the list.

④ Keep pressing `Tab` until the application that you want to use is highlighted.

⑤ Release `⌘`.

The selected application is now in the foreground on the desktop.

TIPS

I have a lot of applications running. Is there a quicker way to switch between them?

To avoid having to cycle all the way around each time you press `Tab`, you can launch the Application Switcher by pressing `⌘` and `Tab` as shown in the steps; then you press `→` or `←` while still holding down `⌘` to move the selection to the right or to the left.

Are there any other ways to quickly switch applications?

Yes. You can press `⌘` and then `Tab` to bring up the Application Switcher. While still holding the `⌘` key down, move the mouse pointer over the icon of the application that you want to use and release the `⌘` key. You can also simply click the icon of any application with a `▢` under it in the Dock.

3

Mastering the Finder

The Finder is an application built in to the Mac OS. It is always running, even when no other applications are running. Almost all computer tasks will somehow involve the Finder. This chapter shows you how to use and customize the Finder so that it fits the way you work.

The Finder is like a home base. Because Mac OS X is a multiuser operating system, each user has his or her own Home folder for personal files and preferences. You can easily access the Home folder in a number of ways, no matter what other folders or applications are open on your system.

FIND THE HOME FOLDER WITH THE MENU BAR

① In the Finder, click **Go**.

② Click **Home**.

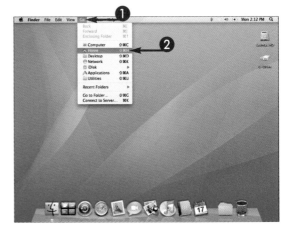

A window opens showing the user's Home folder contents.

③ Press and hold ⌘ and click the Users folder icon at the top of the window.

④ Click **Users**.

The Users folder opens showing all users on this particular computer, but only the current user's Home folder has the Home button (🏠▼).

FIND THE HOME FOLDER FROM THE DESKTOP

1 Click the desktop.

Note: You can click the desktop even with another window or application open.

The Finder application is displayed in the menu bar.

2 Click **File**.

3 Click **New Finder Window**.

A window opens showing the user's Home folder contents.

FIND THE HOME FOLDER FROM ANOTHER OPEN WINDOW

1 With the window open, click on the left.

The user's Home folder window opens.

TIPS

Can I access my Home folder using the Dock?

Yes. You can click the Finder icon (▦) in the Dock at any time and then click ⌂ in the sidebar to open your Home folder. Also, unless you have changed the default preferences in the Finder, clicking in the Finder and pressing ⌘+N will automatically open a Finder window showing the Home folder contents.

Is my Home folder really different from another user's Home folder on the same computer?

Yes. Your Home folder stores all the files that you work on and your personal settings. When you log out, another user cannot alter or erase your files or change any of your personal settings.

Using Contextual Menus

Contextual menus are basically shortcuts to choose commands or perform actions for an active window or a selected item. These specialized menus are easy to access and often contain more information with fewer clicks of the mouse or trackpad than starting from the main menu bar. Using contextual menus can save you time and repetitive wrist actions.

Using Contextual Menus

① Click the desktop.

② Press **Ctrl** and click the desktop again.

Optionally, if you have a multibutton mouse, you can right-click instead of pressing **Ctrl** and clicking.

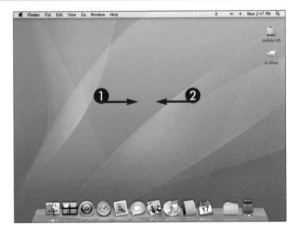

A contextual menu for the Finder appears.

③ Click **New Folder**.

A new folder is created on the desktop.

4 Press Ctrl and click the folder icon.

A contextual menu for the folder appears.

5 Click **Move to Trash**.

The folder disappears from the desktop and is placed in the Trash.

 TIPS

Are the contextual menus the same for all applications?

No. Each application and each different type of file uses contextual menus differently. For example, a Safari Web page displays functions on its contextual menu for saving and printing that page. iTunes displays contextual menu items for songs and playlists. The shortcut menus for regular folders are generally the same.

Are there other types of shortcut menus?

Yes. Some applications, including the Finder, offer Action menus. You can access these shortcuts by clicking the Action button ( ) in the window.

Using the Sidebar

Finder windows open a view into everything on your computer. You can use the sidebar of any Finder window to instantly access the most important locations on your hard drive, as well as any connected and shared drives. By clicking the prebuilt searches, you can quickly find files or recently used applications. You can even add files and applications to the sidebar and launch them with one click.

Using the Sidebar

ADD AN ALIAS TO THE SIDEBAR

1 In the Finder, click **File**.

2 Click **New Finder Window**.

A Finder window opens.

3 Click **Applications**.

The Finder window displays the contents of the Applications folder with the sidebar on the left.

4 Click and drag the icon of the application that you want to add to the sidebar.

An alias for the application appears in the sidebar.

REMOVE AN ALIAS FROM THE SIDEBAR

1 Click and drag the icon from the sidebar to anywhere outside the sidebar.

When you release the mouse button, the application no longer appears in the Finder window sidebar.

TIPS

Does removing an application from the sidebar remove it from my computer?

No. The sidebar, like the Dock, only contains icons representing files, folders, or applications. The original items remain in their respective locations when you add or remove items from the sidebar.

Can I change the size of the sidebar?

Yes. You can click and drag the line separating the sidebar from the rest of the window to change its size.

Customize the Finder

The Finder is your home base. It builds the desktop, or what you see when you turn on the Mac. With Leopard, you can not only customize the appearance of the interface, but you can also personalize the way you sort and organize everything you see.

Using the Finder Preferences dialog box, you can specify what should appear on the desktop, specify how and where a selected folder opens, and change the contents of the sidebar.

USING FINDER PREFERENCES

1 Click **Finder**.

2 Click **Preferences**.

The Finder Preferences dialog box appears.

3 Click **General**.

4 Click to select or deselect the options that you want, such as **Always open folders in a new window**
(☐ changes to ☑).

Note: *You can click to check and uncheck any boxes and move any sliders to suit your individual preferences.*

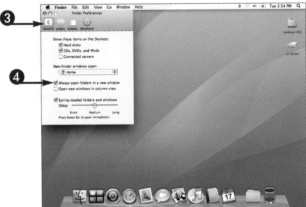

⑤ Click **Sidebar**.

The Sidebar pane of the Finder
Preferences dialog box opens.

⑥ Click to select the items that you want to
appear in the sidebar, such as **Connected
servers** (☐ changes to ☑).

⑦ Click **Advanced**.

The Advanced pane of the Finder
Preferences dialog box opens.

⑧ Click to select the Advanced options that
you want, such as **Show all file
extensions** (☐ changes to ☑).

⑨ Click ⊙ to close the Finder Preferences
dialog box.

Your changes are applied.

What are spring-loaded folders and windows?

When you click and drag an item from one folder to
another, the item is placed at the top level of
organization inside the new folder. If you check **Spring-
loaded folders and windows** on the General pane of
the Finder Preferences dialog box, you can pause as you
drag an item over a folder. The new folder springs open
in a new window revealing its contents. You can hover
over another folder inside the first folder to have it spring
open also. You can then release the mouse button and
place the dragged item specifically where you want.

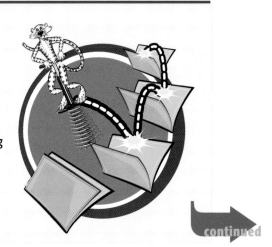

continued

In addition to using the Preferences dialog box, you can use the View menu in the Finder to customize how icons, files, and disks appear on the desktop.

Customize the Finder *(continued)*

USING THE VIEW MENU

① Click  in the Dock.

The Finder window opens in the Cover Flow view.

② Click **View**.

③ Click **as List**.

The Finder window displays the items as a list.

Note: The List view is useful for seeing details about the file or folder and for finding items by date.

● Optionally, you can change the default view by clicking one of the four View buttons in the Finder toolbar.

④ Click **View**.

⑤ Click **as Columns**.

The Finder window displays a column view of its contents.

Note: The Column view enables you to quickly see the folder hierarchy in one window, and selecting an item in Column view displays a preview in a subsequent column.

TIP

What is the toolbar, and how can I customize it?

A toolbar is included at the top of open windows in many applications, including the Finder. Toolbars enable you to quickly access many functions and help you work more efficiently. Clicking **Customize Toolbar** in the View menu opens a window of icons. You can click and drag any icons to the existing Finder window toolbar and place them anywhere you prefer. To rearrange the tools, click and drag them to a different location. You can remove any tool icons by dragging them off the toolbar. You can choose to show the tool icons only or show them with text. To revert to the original toolbar, drag the default set into place.

See All Your Windows with Exposé

Your work area can quickly become cluttered with multiple open windows and applications. Leopard includes a one-click window manager called *Exposé*. When you launch Exposé, it tiles all open windows, making it easy to find and bring to the front the specific window that you want to use. Using Exposé can help you organize your desktop and work more efficiently.

See All Your Windows with Exposé

MANAGE WINDOWS IN THE FINDER

① With many Finder windows open and several applications running, press and release F9.

The background is darkened, and all open windows instantly tile so that you can see all of them at once.

② Move the mouse pointer around the desktop.

Each window becomes highlighted and displays its name as you move the mouse pointer over it.

③ Click a window that you want to work with.

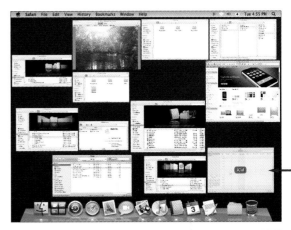

③

The windows return to normal size, the background returns to its normal color, and the selected window appears in the foreground.

TIPS

Why did all my open Finder windows not stay tiled on the desktop when I pressed F9 ?

All the Exposé shortcut keys can be used as a toggle or as a momentary switch. When you tap or press the key briefly, the windows will tile. When you press and hold the key, the windows tile, but immediately return to the previous state when you let go.

Can I slow down the Exposé animation?

If you press and hold Shift before pressing any of the Exposé shortcut keys F9 , F10 , and F11 , the animation moves in slow motion.

continued

Exposé actually has three different functions, each controlled by a separate keystroke. You can display all the open windows of all running applications by pressing F9 as shown previously. You can also display all the open windows in one application to find the one that you want to work with. A third keystroke temporarily clears the desktop.

See All Your Windows with Exposé *(continued)*

MANAGE WINDOWS IN RUNNING APPLICATIONS

1 With a number of windows open in one application, press `F10`.

Note: *Several applications can also be running; however, pressing* `F10` *only highlights the windows of the frontmost application.*

All open windows instantly resize and reposition so that you can see each one. Only the ones in the application that was open in the menu bar are highlighted.

2 Move the mouse pointer around the desktop.

Each window becomes highlighted and displays its name as you move the mouse pointer over it.

3 Click the window that you want to work with.

The windows return to normal size with
the selected window in the foreground.

CLEAR THE DESKTOP

 ① Press F11.

All the windows slide off to the sides of the
screen, clearing the desktop.

② Press F11 again.

All the windows slide back into their
original positions.

TIP

Does Exposé have any other uses?

Exposé can help you move and copy items more easily from one
window to another location, especially if you have many
windows open. For example, when you cannot see the desktop
but need to move an item there, click and start to drag the item.
Press F11 to hide all the windows and reveal the desktop. With
the item hovering over the desktop, release the mouse button.
To copy rather than move the item, simply press Option before
releasing the mouse button. If you simply want an alias of the
item on the desktop, press ⌘+Option before releasing the
mouse button.

Get Information about Files

The Finder stores numerous details about the files that you create. By opening the Get Info dialog box, you can access information regarding the file size, the creation or modification dates, and where the file is located on your computer. You can also make useful changes to how files appear or open.

① In the Finder, click a file.

② Click **File**.

③ Click **Get Info**.

The Info dialog box opens, displaying the details about the file.

④ Click the More Info ▶.

The window enlarges, showing context-sensitive information, such as the dimensions of a JPEG or when the file was last opened.

Note: *The details in More Info change depending on the type of file selected.*

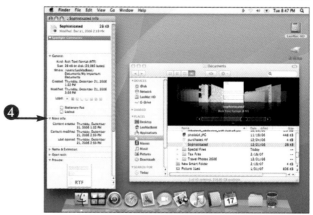

⑤ Click the Open With ▶.

The application currently set to open the file is displayed.

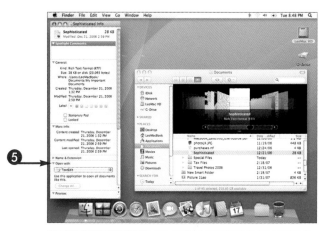

⑥ Click ⬍ to select a different application.

Note: *The applications listed depend on the type of file selected.*

TIPS

What are Spotlight comments?
Spotlight comments act like tags for your files. You can type words to help you find the files more quickly later in the Spotlight Comments data field of the Get Info dialog box. For example, you can add a project name. When you search using Spotlight, all the files with the project tag will be listed together.

Can I change a filename in the Name & Extension section of the Get Info dialog box?
Yes. You can type a new name in the data field. You can also choose to show the extension, listed as a dot followed usually by three letters, by clicking the box next to **Hide Extension** (☑ changes to ☐). However, it is best not to change the original extension because many applications require specific file type extensions to open files.

Get Information about Your Mac and System

You can quickly find detailed information about your computer and operating system by using the System Profiler built in to the Mac OS. You can find out what hardware and software are installed; the computer serial number; the types of CD, DVD, or other drives attached; the types of other peripheral devices; and how much memory your computer has installed.

Get Information about Your Mac and System

① Click .

② Click **About This Mac**.

A dialog box appears showing the Mac OS X version, the processor type, and amount of memory.

③ Click **More Info**.

The System Profiler utility launches, and a window opens that displays the characteristics of the computer.

④ Click the ▶ next to an item about which you want more information, such as **Hardware**.

The list expands.

⑤ Click a subtopic about which you want system details, such as **Disc Burning**.

In this example, the technical details of the CD or DVD drive are listed on the right pane in the window.

Why do I need to see details about my computer and operating system?

If you ever need to call Apple support for technical assistance, the agent may ask you for some details about your hardware and software. The information regarding your computer and operating system is useful in diagnosing and solving technical problems when they arise. Also, because various applications require specific amounts of RAM, you may need to check your computer's memory to determine if you can install and run the application or if you need to install more memory. The System Profiler is also useful for quickly identifying the versions and kinds of software that you have installed because it scans all the applications and other software on your computer and lists these in groups.

Customize Icons

The Mac interface has always included icons to represent each tool, application, folder, and file. Applications come with specially designed icons to help you recognize them quickly. Many file icons and almost all folder icons, however, look the same. Leopard enables you to change the icons of folders and files for easy recognition or just to personalize your Mac.

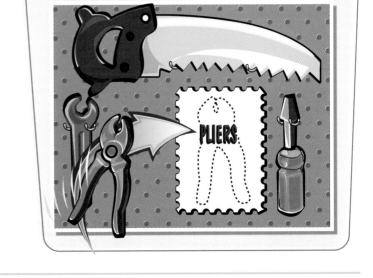

Customize Icons

① In any Finder window, click a file or folder whose icon you want to use for another item's icon.

② Click **File**.

③ Click **Get Info**.

An Info dialog box opens.

④ Click the icon in the Info window to select it.

⑤ Click **Edit**.

⑥ Click **Copy**.

A copy of the icon is saved in the background to the Clipboard.

⑦ In the Finder, click the file or folder whose icon you want to change.

⑧ Repeat steps **2** to **3**.

An Info dialog box opens.

⑨ Click the icon in the Info dialog box to select it.

⑩ Click **Edit**.

⑪ Click **Paste**.

● The icon of the destination file changes to match the source icon.

TIPS

Where can I find different icons to use for my files and folders?

You can copy any existing icons from files or folders on your computer or copy and paste most photos such as those from a digital camera. You can also find free icons at various Web sites on the Internet, such as the Iconfactory at www.iconfactory.com, InterfaceLIFT at www.interfacelift.com/icons-mac, and Pixelgirl Presents at www.pixelgirlpresents.com/icons.php.

Can I change the icons of any of my files and folders?

You can change the icon as long as you have write access under the Sharing & Permissions section at the bottom of the Info dialog box for that file or folder. Click ▶ by Sharing and Permissions. If it states that you can **Read and Write**, then you can change the icon.

Color-Code Your Files and Folders

Your Mac stores many files, folders, tools, and applications on the hard drive. As you add applications and create new files and folders, finding a specific item becomes more difficult. Leopard enables you to color-code items for quicker visual recognition, so you can work more efficiently.

Color-Code Your Files and Folders

ADD A COLORED LABEL

1 Open a Finder window.

2 Click the file or folder to which you want to add a colored label.

3 Click **File**.

4 Click a colored square under the Label category.

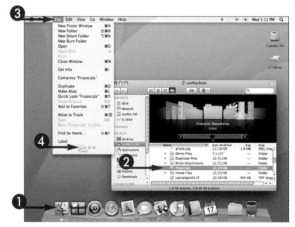

● The color is automatically applied to the file or folder name.

Note: *You can sort files and folders in Icon view using the colored labels by clicking* **View → Arrange By → Label***.*

REMOVE A COLORED LABEL

1. Click the file or folder to select it.

2. Click **File**.

3. Click ⊠ under the Label category.

● The color is removed from the file or folder name.

 TIPS

How do I apply a colored label to multiple files or folders at one time?

Press and hold ⌘ as you click a number of folders to select them all at once. Then apply the colored label as shown here. You can remove multiple colored labels, even a mixture of labels, by pressing ⌘ and clicking the folders to select them. Then remove the colored labels also as shown in these steps.

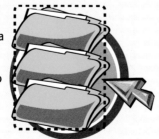

Can I change the words associated with the colored labels?

Yes. Click 🖥 in the Dock or click the desktop to open the Finder. In the menu, click **Finder →Preferences**. In the Finder Preferences window, click **Labels**. Double-click any of the color names and type the name that you prefer. By giving different names to each color, you can further categorize your folders.

Duplicate Files

Making a copy of a file or folder is essential for safeguarding and sharing your projects. By working on a copy, you do not alter the original. You can duplicate important files and folders to share with others and as part of a backup system for safekeeping. You can duplicate files and folders four different ways, as shown here.

COPY A FILE WITH A MENU

1 In the Finder or in a Finder window, click the file that you want to duplicate.

2 Click **File**.

3 Click **Duplicate**.

The Finder makes a copy of the file in the same location and adds the word *copy* to the name.

Note: *If you duplicate a file with* copy *in the name, the duplicate is named* copy 2.

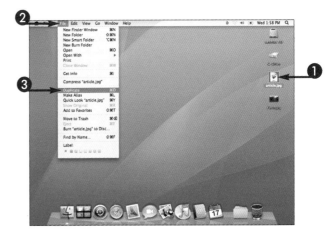

COPY A FILE WITH A KEYBOARD SHORTCUT

1 In the Finder, click the file that you want to duplicate.

2 Press ⌘+D.

● The Finder makes a copy of the file in the same location and adds the word *copy* to the name.

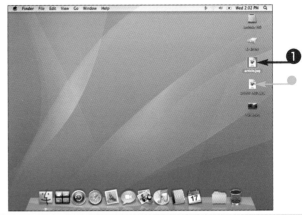

COPY A FILE TO ANOTHER LOCATION USING COPY AND PASTE

1 In the Finder or in a window, click the file that you want to duplicate.

2 Click **Edit**.

3 Click **Copy *filename***.

4 Double-click a folder or other location where you want to place a copy of the file.

Note: Double-clicking opens the folder.

5 Click **Edit**.

6 Click **Paste Item**.

The Finder makes a copy of the file in the new location.

COPY A FILE TO ANOTHER LOCATION USING DRAG AND DROP

1 On the desktop or in a window, click the file that you want to duplicate.

2 Press and hold Option.

3 Click and drag the file to another location on the desktop or over another folder.

The Finder makes a copy of the file in the new location.

 TIPS

How do I copy a file from one hard drive to another disk drive attached to my computer?

Click and drag the file or folder from the source disk drive to the new location. The Finder automatically makes a copy because the file or folder is moved to a different disk drive. ⓑ indicates that a duplicate is placed in a new location.

Why did my original file disappear when I clicked and dragged it to another folder?

If you click and drag a file from one location to another on the same disk drive, the Finder simply moves the file to the new location. Pressing Option before clicking and dragging a file or folder from one location to another on the same disk tells the Finder that you want to duplicate it and not just move it.

Delete Files

Like traditional files, you will delete files at different times. You can delete files using menus or by clicking and dragging a file directly to the Trash icon in the Dock. However, the file is not removed from your hard drive until you intentionally empty the Trash.

Delete Files

DELETE USING THE FINDER MENU

1. In the Finder or any window, click a file to delete.

2. Click **File**.

3. Click **Move to Trash**.

   The Finder moves the file to the Trash.

DELETE USING CONTEXTUAL MENUS

1. Press and hold Control.

2. Click a file to delete.

3. Click **Move to Trash**.

   The Finder moves the file to the Trash.

DELETE BY CLICKING AND DRAGGING

1 Click a file to delete.

2 Drag the file over the Trash icon (🗑) in the Dock.

3 Release the mouse button.

The Trash icon appears filled.

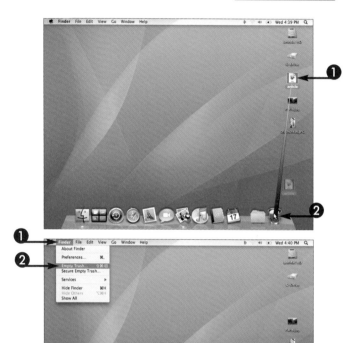

EMPTY THE TRASH

1 Click **Finder**.

2 Click **Empty Trash**.

The Finder permanently removes the files from the Trash.

Note: *If you have the sound effect on, you will hear a crunching sound.*

Are there any keyboard shortcuts for deleting files?

You can quickly move any file to the Trash by clicking the file to select it and pressing ⌘+ Delete . You can also empty the Trash using a keyboard shortcut. In the Finder, press ⌘+ Shift + Delete .

What is the difference between Empty Trash and Secure Empty Trash in the Finder menu?

When you click **Empty Trash**, the Finder does not actually erase the files. Instead it marks the areas on your disk where those files resided as safe to overwrite when the Mac OS requires more disk space. Secure Empty Trash really does erase the files by writing over the location on the disk with random data, making it unrecoverable by ordinary means.

Using Keyboard Shortcuts

You can perform many tasks on your computer by pressing keys on the keyboard. Some shortcuts work the same way in all applications; others apply only to one application. Learning to use common keyboard shortcuts can save you time and make you more proficient with the computer interface.

Using Keyboard Shortcuts

OPEN THE APPLICATIONS WINDOW

① In the Finder, press ⌘ + Shift + A.

The Applications window opens.

SELECT AN APPLICATION

② Press Tab once.

The first listed application is highlighted.

③ Press Tab a number of times until the application that you want to use is highlighted.

OPEN AN APPLICATION

④ Press ⌘ + O.

The selected application launches.

OPEN A NEW INSTANCE

⑤ Press ⌘ + N.

● In this example, iCal creates a new event.

Note: ⌘ + N *opens something new depending on the application. For example, it can open a new window in the Finder or a new document in a text editor.*

CLOSE A WINDOW

❻ With a window selected, press ⌘ + W.

The application's window closes.

Note: *Pressing* ⌘ + Option + W *closes all open windows in an application at once.*

EXIT AN APPLICATION

❼ Press ⌘ + Q.

The application quits.

TIPS

Are there other basic keyboard shortcuts that I should know?

When the Finder opens a dialog box with the OK button highlighted, you can press Return or Enter instead of clicking **OK**. For that same type of dialog box, pressing Esc is the same as clicking **Cancel**.

Where can I find the keys for other keyboard shortcuts?

The menus of the Finder or any application always show any existing keyboard shortcuts associated with a menu command. You can also find a list of your existing keyboard shortcuts by clicking **System Preferences** under and clicking **Keyboard & Mouse**. Click the **Keyboard Shortcuts** tab to see the current keyboard shortcuts.

You can compress files to save disk space and to transfer them more easily in emails and over the Internet. When you compress a file or folder, the Finder makes a copy of the item or items and places the compressed duplicate in the same location as the original file. The compressed file has a new zippered icon and the extension .zip.

Compress Files

COMPRESS A FILE

❶ Click a file to compress on the desktop or in a window.

❷ Click **File**.

❸ Click **Compress *filename***.

● The compressed file with the extension .zip appears in the same location.

COMPRESS A FILE WITH A CONTEXTUAL MENU

❶ In the Finder or a window, press and hold Ctrl.

❷ Click the file that you want to compress.

❸ Click **Compress *filename***.

● The Finder compresses the file and
appends the .zip extension to the
filename.

EXTRACT A COMPRESSED FILE

① Double-click the compressed file or folder.

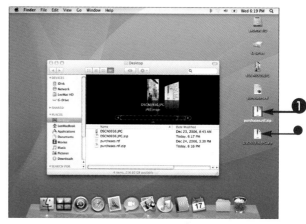

● The Finder extracts the data from the
compressed file and restores it to its
original state.

TIPS

Can I select a number of items to compress at the same time??

Press ⌘ as you click any number of items to
select them. When you click **File → Compress
number Items**, the Finder copies
and groups them all into a
.zip file with the name
Archive.zip. If you place
all the separate items
into a folder with a name,
you can compress the
folder, and that archive will
maintain the name of the folder.

How much space can I save by compressing a file?

The space saved varies with the type of file that
you compress — from more than 90 percent to as
little as nothing. Text files and
folders of text files generally
compress more than image
files. Because file formats
such as MP3 and JPEG files
are already compressed,
compressing such files does
not save much space.

Take a Quick Look at Your Files

You can easily preview the contents of almost any file without opening it or the associated application by using Leopard's new feature called Quick Look. You can access Quick Look from any Finder window and in any View mode.

Take a Quick Look at Your Files

① Click ⬛ in the Dock.

A new Finder window appears.

② Click a file to select it.

③ Click here to open the file in Quick Look.

The file appears in a new window.

Note: If the file is a video or movie file, it starts playing.

④ Click here to view the file in full-screen mode.

The file fills the screen.

5 Click here to return to the smaller Quick Look view.

● Optionally, you can click the X to close the Quick Look view.

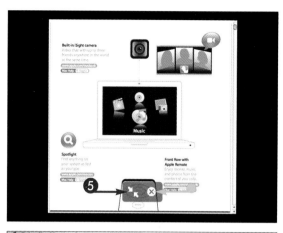

The Quick Look window returns to the small size.

6 Click here to close the Quick Look view.

 TIPS

Are there any keyboard shortcuts for using Quick Look?

Yes. Click a file to select it in any of the four view modes. Tap Spacebar to view the file with Quick Look. You can also press Shift +click a sequential group of files or ⌘ +click multiple files and press Spacebar to open them with Quick Look. Then press the arrow keys to cycle through the selected files.

Can I use Quick Look to find a specific page of a multipage document?

Yes. Quick Look lets you look through an entire file and flip through the pages of multipage documents. You can click and drag the scrollbar in the small view, or if you are in full-screen mode, tap Spacebar to turn the pages.

Customizing Leopard

A Macintosh is a computer with personality. You can customize the look of the screen and how the features in the Finder operate. You can adjust colors, screen savers, keyboard shortcuts, and more to fit your personality and your work. Customizing your Mac makes your computer time more efficient and more fun.

Understanding Preferences

Preferences are the keys to all the customizable settings in Mac OS X. Whether you install Leopard or if your computer came with Leopard preinstalled, the preferences for various aspects of the system use the default settings. You can change these settings and customize not only the interface but also how the computer responds to your input.

System Preferences

The System Preferences are the main control center of Mac OS X Leopard. Most of the options such as desktop appearance, utility settings such as date and time, and connectivity settings for networking and external hardware can be found in the System Preferences window.

System Preferences Window

The System Preferences window is divided into separate sections, including Personal, Hardware, Internet & Network, and System. A search field at the top of the window enables you to type keywords to quickly find the corresponding icons that are then spotlighted. A drop-down menu also lists specific options related to your search.

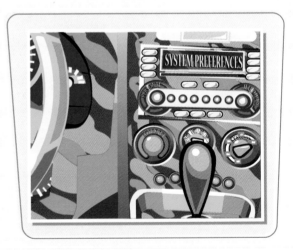

Individual Preferences

Clicking an icon in the System Preferences window opens the Preferences pane for that item with a number of different options. For example, the Displays dialog box enables you to change both the display resolution and the color profile for your monitor.

Change Your Mac Anytime

Mac OS X Leopard can be adjusted anytime. You can set preferences and change them if you change your mind. Your settings are applied immediately, so you can change your preferences whenever you change your style.

Application Preferences

Each application has its own set of preferences. Application Preferences are generally accessed in the application's menu under the name of the application. For example, you can click Mail with the Mail application running and click Preferences to open the Mail Preferences window.

Additional Preferences

Certain input devices or other external hardware, as well as some software applications, add their own icon to the System Preferences window. These new preferences are classified in a category called Other.

Change the Appearance of the Mac Interface

You can personalize your desktop as you would a traditional desktop by selecting your own color schemes. Changing the text highlight color may seem insignificant; however, it enables you to find items much more quickly.

In the Appearance Preferences window, you can also customize window scrolling and text smoothing.

Change the Appearance of the Mac Interface

① Click .

② Click **System Preferences**.

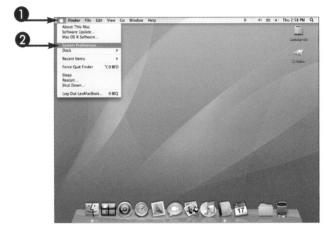

The System Preferences window opens.

③ Click **Appearance**.

The Appearance window opens.

4 Click and click **Gold**.

Any highlighted text will now be more visible in gold.

Note: *Changing the Appearance color from Blue to Graphite changes the look of buttons, menus, and windows to gray.*

5 Click **At top and bottom** (○ changes to ◉).

Scroll arrows will now be placed at the top and bottom of the scrollbar.

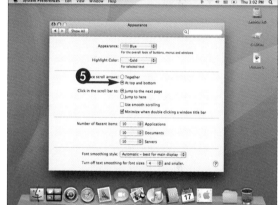

TIPS

What do the Number of Recent Items settings in the Appearance window control?

The Number of Recent Items settings refer to the Recent Items selection listed under the in the menu bar. You can select how many recently accessed applications, documents, and servers you want to see when you click → **Recent Items**.

Why would I want to turn off text smoothing?

Mac OS X Leopard adds a certain amount of fuzziness to display fonts to make the curves in letters look good. With very small font sizes, the smoothing can sometimes make the text less legible. Using the Appearance window, you can force Leopard to remove the smoothing for small fonts depending on your monitor. Generally fonts smaller than 8 points look best without smoothing applied.

Customize Your Desktop Background

The desktop background is always visible in the Finder. In fact, it is visible almost all the time. You can replace the default green grass and add your own personal touch to the desktop using the Desktop & Screen Saver Preferences window.

CHANGE THE DESKTOP BACKGROUND

① In the System Preferences window, click **Desktop & Screen Saver**.

Note: *To view the System Preferences window, see the previous section, "Change the Appearance of the Mac Interface."*

The Desktop tab of the Desktop & Screen Saver window opens.

② Click a category of background images, such as **Apple Images**.

The right side of the window displays thumbnails of the included images in that category.

③ Click an image.

The desktop background changes to your selection.

USE A PERSONAL PHOTO BACKGROUND

① Click **Pictures Folder** on the Desktop tab of the Desktop & Screen Saver window.

Note: The Pictures folder is located in your Home folder and contains any images you placed there from iPhoto or another photo application.

② Click an image thumbnail.

The photo becomes your desktop background.

③ Click 🔽 and select **Fill Screen**.

The image resizes to cover the entire desktop.

HAVE YOUR PHOTO BACKGROUND CHANGE PERIODICALLY

① Click **Change Picture** (☐ changes to ☑).

② Click 🔽 and select a time interval.

The desktop background changes images and transitions to the next one after the selected time delay.

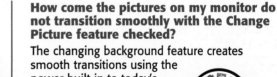

 TIPS

What is the best background for viewing photos?

If you are editing photos, whether from iPhoto or another application, it is best to have a neutral, solid-colored background. Click **Solid Colors** in the Desktop Preferences pane and select either **Solid Gray** or **Solid Gray Medium**.

How come the pictures on my monitor do not transition smoothly with the Change Picture feature checked?

The changing background feature creates smooth transitions using the power built in to today's advanced video cards. You may see a slight delay when pictures change, depending on the video card in your computer. You can decrease the delay by increasing the time between picture changes.

Select a Screen Saver

You can hide the items on your desktop when you walk away from your computer by using a screen saver. Screen saver images can be static, or they can fill the screen with mesmerizing computer animations. The Mac OS System Preferences enable you to select not only which images are displayed but also how they are displayed.

Select a Screen Saver

① In the System Preferences window, click **Desktop & Screen Saver**.

Note: To view the System Preferences window, see the section "Change the Appearance of the Mac Interface" earlier in this chapter.

The Desktop & Screen Saver window opens.

② Click **Screen Saver**.

The screen savers are listed on the left with a Preview window on the right.

● You can scroll to see more screen savers.

③ Click a screen saver in the list.

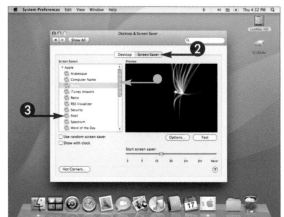

The selected screen saver starts playing in the Preview window.

④ Click **Test**.

The desktop first goes black, and then the screen saver runs in full-screen preview mode.

⑤ Click anywhere on the display or move the cursor to stop the screen saver.

The desktop reappears with the Desktop & Screen Saver System Preferences window open.

 TIP

What do the Start Screen Saver slider and Hot Corners button do?

Using the Start Screen Saver slider, you can set the amount of time the computer is inactive before the screen saver automatically starts. You can also set up a specific corner on the display to start or stop the screen saver. You click **Hot Corners**, select a corner, and then select an action such as **Start** or **Disable Screen Saver** from the pop-up menu. Click **OK**. You can then drag the mouse to that corner of your monitor to activate or deactivate the screen saver anytime.

The Dock is a great place to keep icons of frequently used applications, Internet and email downloads, and files. You can launch applications from the Dock and also use it to temporarily store minimized open windows. Customizing the Dock makes it even more useful.

Personalize the Dock

OPEN DOCK PREFERENCES

1 In the System Preferences window, click **Dock**.

Note: *To view the System Preferences window, see the section "Change the Appearance of the Mac Interface" earlier in this chapter.*

   The Dock window appears.

CHANGE THE DOCK SIZE

1 Click and drag the Size ⊜ left to decrease the Dock's size and right to increase the size.

   The Dock changes in size.

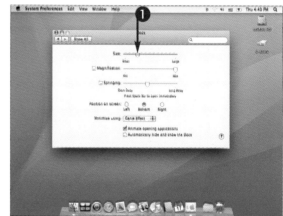

CHANGE THE DOCK MAGNIFICATION

1 Click **Magnification** (changes to).

2 Click and drag the Magnification
toward **Max**.

● The Dock icons increase in size as you
move the mouse pointer over them.

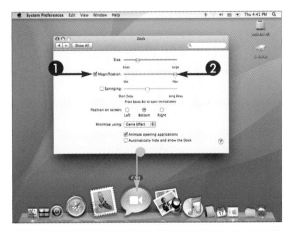

REPOSITION THE DOCK

1 Click **Left** or **Right** (changes to).

The Dock moves to the left or right edge
of the screen.

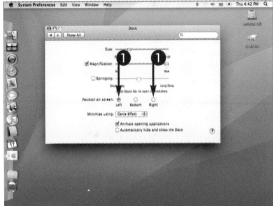

TIPS

**What does Minimize Using Scale Effect or
Minimize Using Genie Effect do?**

Clicking the Minimize button ( ) on an open
window temporarily hides the window and stores
it in the Dock. With Minimize Using Scale Effect
selected in the Dock Preferences, the
window shrinks down to icon size
in the Dock. With Minimize
Using Genie Effect selected,
the window flows down
into the Dock like a genie
going into a magic lamp.
You can view these effects
in slow motion by pressing
Shift while clicking in an
open window.

**Why do some icons in my Dock have a
under them?**

The indicates that an application is
running. Some applications are in
the Dock when you first open the
Mac OS. Whenever you launch
an application, its icon is
automatically but
temporarily added to the
Dock. You can also add icons
of frequently used applications
to the Dock; see Chapter 2 for
information on how to do so.

Set Up a Corner to Activate Viewing All Windows in Exposé

When you work on various projects, you can have many windows open on the desktop. You can use the Exposé feature in Mac OS X to quickly clear the clutter with a mouse click in one corner and find the window that you need.

Set Up a Corner to Activate Viewing All Windows in Exposé

① In the System Preferences window, click **Exposé & Spaces**.

Note: To view the System Preferences window, see the section "Change the Appearance of the Mac Interface" earlier in this chapter.

The Exposé & Spaces window appears.

② Click this ▼ and select **All Windows**.

③ Move the cursor over the bottom-right corner of the screen.

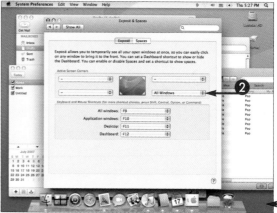

All the open windows separate so that they are all viewable at once.

④ Move the cursor over one of the open windows and click to bring it to the front.

Note: You can also move the cursor back over the bottom-right corner to return the windows to their original position.

The windows return to their original stacked position.

TIPS

What does the desktop shortcut F11 do?

Pressing F11, or setting one of the Active Screen Corners ⬦ to **Desktop**, enables you to quickly access the desktop no matter how many windows are open. F11 moves all the open windows just off the screen, giving you complete access to the desktop and Finder.

Can I change the default shortcut keys?

Yes, however, because there are so many preassigned keyboard shortcuts, it is best to learn and use the default keys for the basic interface items. You can always change them later if you need to speed up access for a specific application.

Display the Keyboard Viewer

The keyboard for your computer shows the characters for the principal language that you use. However, you may sometimes type words or phrases in other languages or may need to use specific symbols for particular projects. The Keyboard Viewer is a small utility that enables you to see what keys to type in a specific font for accented letters or special characters.

Display the Keyboard Viewer

① In the System Preferences window, click **International**.

Note: To view the System Preferences window, see the section "Change the Appearance of the Mac Interface" earlier in this chapter.

The International window appears, displaying all the installed keyboard layouts.

② Click **Input Menu**.

③ Click **Keyboard Viewer** (☐ changes to ☑).

④ Click **Show input menu in menu bar** (☐ changes to ☑).

A 🖼 denoting the main language appears in the menu bar on the right.

⑤ Click 🖼.

⑥ Click **Show Keyboard Viewer**.

The Keyboard Viewer appears, displaying a virtual keyboard.

⑦ Press Option to view the some of the other available characters on the keyboard.

The characters on the keyboard change, and the accented characters are highlighted in orange.

Note: *You can also press other modifier keys such as* Ctrl, ⌘, *and* Shift *to display other available keyboard characters.*

 TIPS

How do I type an accented character?

With the text document open and your font selected, open the Keyboard Viewer as shown here. Press Option and click the accented key on the virtual keyboard once. Release Option and click the appropriate letter on the actual keyboard. After you learn where the accented characters are, you can use them without opening the Keyboard Viewer.

Why do some keys have missing characters?

The Keyboard Viewer displays the characters specific to the currently selected font. Not all fonts include all the possible accents, symbols, or characters.

Speed Up Your Spotlight Searches

The Spotlight feature in Mac OS X Leopard enables you to search for any file anywhere on your computer using a keyword or any words associated with the file, folder, or application. You can even use Spotlight to search other Macs or servers connected to your computer. You can speed up your searches by specifying search categories and reducing the number of folders for searching in the Spotlight Preferences.

Speed Up Your Spotlight Searches

① In the System Preferences window, click **Spotlight**.

Note: To view the System Preferences window, see the section "Change the Appearance of the Mac Interface" earlier in this chapter.

The Spotlight Preferences appear.

② Click and drag **System Preferences** to the bottom of the list.

Note: You can click and drag the search items into any order.

③ Click **Fonts**(☑ changes to ☐).

Note: Spotlight will no longer search through the installed fonts.

④ Click **Privacy**.

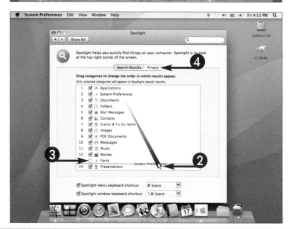

An empty window pane appears.

5 Click [+].

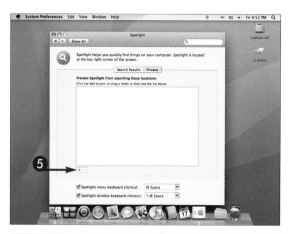

A hierarchical display of your Home folder appears.

6 Click any folder to prevent it from being searched.

7 Click **Choose**.

The selected folder appears in the list pane, indicating that Spotlight will not search that location.

Note: *The fewer folders that Spotlight has to search through, the faster its search time will be.*

Can I stop Spotlight from searching an attached external hard drive?

Yes. Click and drag the icon of the attached hard drive to the Privacy window pane.

Is there a fast way to open the document that I found using Spotlight?

Yes. A Spotlight feature of Mac OS X Leopard is that it can act as an application launcher. Spotlight lists the items that it finds and highlights the top one. Click, or double-click in some windows, the item that you want in the list to launch the appropriate application and open the file.

Make Bluetooth Devices Interact with Your Mac

Bluetooth is a short-range wireless technology that lets you connect enabled items within a 30-foot range. If your Macintosh hardware has Bluetooth capability, you can connect your Mac without cables to Bluetooth-enabled devices such as mobile phones, keyboards, and mice. Using the Bluetooth Preferences, which appear only with a Bluetooth-enabled Mac, you can control how your computer and wireless peripherals communicate.

Make Bluetooth Devices Interact with Your Mac

① In the System Preferences window, click **Bluetooth**.

Note: *To view the System Preferences window, see the section "Change the Appearance of the Mac Interface" earlier in this chapter.*

The Bluetooth Preferences appear.

② Click **Bluetooth Off** (☐ changes to ☑).

③ Click **Discoverable** (☐ changes to ☑).

④ Click **Show Bluetooth status in the menu bar** (☐ changes to ☑).

Note: *Your settings may already have been set with Bluetooth and Discoverable turned on and the Bluetooth status icon in the menu bar.*

5 Click **Set Up New Device**.

● Optionally, you can click ⊞.

The Bluetooth Setup Assistant appears.

6 Click **Continue** and follow the online steps to connect your particular Bluetooth-enabled device.

Can I add Bluetooth capabilities to an older Macintosh?

Yes. You can enable some previous generation iBooks, iMacs, or Power Macs by purchasing an adapter such as the D-Link Bluetooth USB Adapter. The adapter plugs into a free USB port on your computer or keyboard.

Is it possible to send documents to a printer with Bluetooth?

Yes. If your Macintosh has Bluetooth and your printer is designed to support Bluetooth, you can set up your Bluetooth Preferences to send documents to the printer wirelessly.

Set the Default Behaviors of CDs and DVDs

You can predetermine how your Mac responds when you insert a CD or DVD. For example, you can have it launch a related application or ask you what to do with the disc. By controlling the default behavior using the settings in the CDs & DVDs pane of System Preferences, you can make your computing time more efficient.

Set the Default Behaviors of CDs and DVDs

① In the System Preferences window, click **CDs & DVDs**.

Note: *To view the System Preferences window, see the section "Change the Appearance of the Mac Interface" earlier in this chapter.*

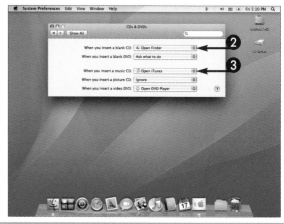

The CDs &DVDs Preferences pane opens.

② Click this ▼ and select **Open Finder**.

Blank CDs will now appear in the Finder just like any other disc.

③ Click this ▼ and select **Open iTunes**.

When you insert a music CD, the iTunes application will launch.

④ Click this ⬍ and select **Open other application**.

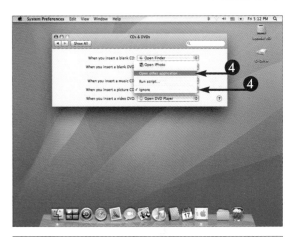

The Applications folder opens.

⑤ Click **iPhoto** or another photo application.

⑥ Click **Choose**.

All photo CDs will now open automatically with iPhoto or the selected application.

Can I set the Mac to launch another application for disc burning?

Yes. You can select **Open other application** as the choice when you insert a blank CD or DVD. The Applications folder opens, and you can then select a third-party disc utility that you have installed, such as Roxio Toast or NTI Dragon Burn.

How do I erase CD-RW and DVD-RW discs?

You can erase optical media using the Disk Utility application. You can find it in the Utilities folder located in the Applications folder of your hard drive. You can also erase such discs with third-party disc-burning applications. Erasing a rewritable CD or DVD can take time, so be patient while the process takes place.

Adjust the Display Settings

Whether your Mac has a separate monitor or one that is built in, you can adjust the display settings for the aspect ratios that best suit your monitor and your application. You can also adjust the color using the built-in Display Calibrator Assistant or use a color profile that you create with a third-party application.

Adjust the Display Settings

① In the System Preferences window, click **Displays**.

Note: To view the System Preferences window, see the section "Change the Appearance of the Mac Interface" earlier in this chapter.

The Displays Preferences pane opens.

● The type of monitor that you have is the name of the window.

② Click a dimension in the Resolutions list.

Note: If you have more than one display attached, each display screen shows a window, and the main display screen includes an Arrangement tab.

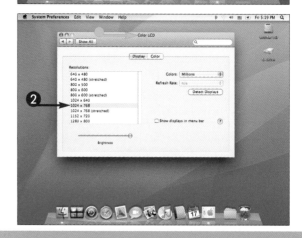

The display switches to the resolution that you selected.

③ Click **Show displays in menu bar** (☐ changes to ☑).

● A small icon of a display (🖥) appears in the menu bar.

TIPS

Why should I keep the 🖥 icon in the menu bar?

The monitor is your window into the computer. You should check the display resolution and color, especially when you connect another monitor or if you attach a projector to the computer. You may also want to recalibrate the color before you adjust photos and graphics.

What does the Detect Displays button on the Display tab do?

If you have more than one monitor attached, Detect Displays shows you each monitor with a number on it. The display with the number 1 is the principal monitor and will show the menu bar.

continued

Color calibration is a sophisticated process, and third-party applications are most often used when accurate color is critical. However, you can get good results for general computer use with the built-in Display Calibrator Assistant feature of the Mac OS X by following certain guidelines.

Adjust the Display Settings *(continued)*

④ Click **Color**.

The Color Preferences pane opens.

● The currently running color profile is highlighted.

⑤ Click **Calibrate**.

The Display Calibrator Assistant appears.

⑥ Click **Continue**.

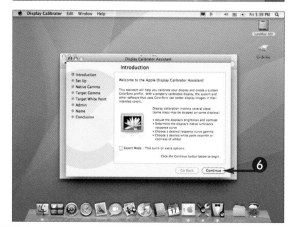

The assistant guides you through the calibration process and creates a color profile.

7 Name the profile using the date in the final window.

Note: All displays lose color accuracy over time. Date the color profile to help you determine when the profile is getting old.

8 Click **Continue**.

9 Click **Done** in the last Calibrator window.

● The profile is listed and highlighted under Display Profile.

What can I do to create a more accurate color profile?

Click **Expert Mode** (☐ changes to ☑) on the Introduction screen of the Display Calibrator Assistant. The assistant offers the viewer more control over the settings during the process. Also, because the ambient light and reflections on the screen can alter the monitor profile, follow these rules as you use the assistant in Expert mode or with external hardware colorimeters and software:

● Wear a neutral color such as gray or black when you are in front of the screen.

● Make sure that no outside lights or window light are reflecting on the monitor.

● Dim the lights in the room.

Using the Energy Saver pane of System Preferences, you can adjust settings that put your computer to sleep, cause the display to sleep, and even spin down the hard drive. This can be useful especially for laptop users when running on battery because you can set the sleep preferences for both power adapter use and when using battery power.

Schedule Sleep

1 In System Preferences, click **Energy Saver**.

Note: *To view the System Preferences window, see the section "Change the Appearance of the Mac Interface" earlier in this chapter.*

The Energy Saver pane opens.

2 Click **Show Details**.

The window lengthens.

③ Click the Settings For ⟰ and select a power source.

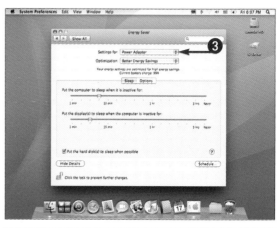

④ Click the Optimization ⟰ and select **Custom**.

⑤ Click and drag this ◎ to adjust the computer sleep timer.

The computer will sleep after a period of inactivity based on this setting.

⑥ Click and drag this ◎ to adjust the display sleep timer.

The display will sleep after a period of inactivity based on this setting.

 TIPS

What is on the Options tab of the Energy Saver window?

Clicking **Options** opens another pane with specific selections. Laptop users should check **Show battery status in the menu bar** (◻ changes to ☑) because this enables you to constantly monitor the remaining power when running on battery.

What does the Schedule button do?

You can schedule specific startup and shutdown times using the Energy Saver Preferences. Click **Schedule** and in the open dialog box, click **Startup or wake** and **Shut Down**. Set the time and day for these actions, and the computer will start up and shut down automatically on schedule.

Adjust the Keyboard and Mouse

You can customize the feel of both your keyboard and mouse. Using the Keyboard & Mouse Preferences, you can change the typing speed for repeat letters and the tracking speed and the double-click speed for the mouse. You can also control the settings for a laptop Mac's trackpad.

The Keyboard & Mouse Preferences window is also used to view or change keyboard shortcuts.

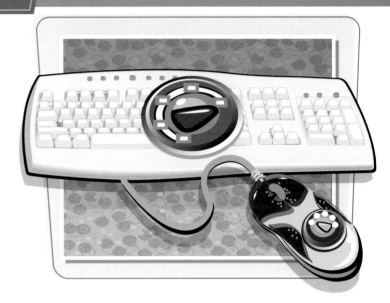

Adjust the Keyboard and Mouse

① In System Preferences, click **Keyboard & Mouse**.

Note: *To view the System Preferences window, see the section "Change the Appearance of the Mac Interface" earlier in this chapter.*

The Keyboard & Mouse pane opens.

② Click **Keyboard**.

③ Click and drag this 🔘 to change how rapidly repeated letters appear when a key is continuously depressed.

④ Click and drag this 🔘 to change the delay before a depressed key produces multiple characters on the screen.

⑤ Click **Mouse**.

Note: *If you have a laptop Mac without a separate mouse attached, the Mouse option is not available.*

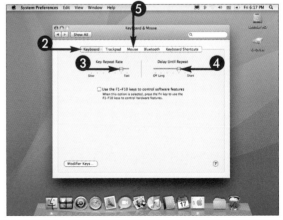

The Mouse Preferences options appear.

6 Click and drag this 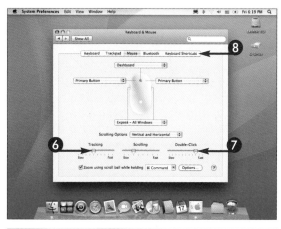 to change how quickly the onscreen pointer tracks when the mouse is moved.

7 Click and drag this to modify how rapidly you must click the mouse for the computer to recognize a double-click.

8 Click **Keyboard Shortcuts**.

A listing of systemwide keyboard shortcuts appears.

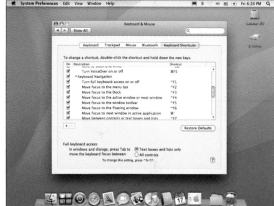

TIPS

Can I add my own keyboard shortcuts?

Yes. First click ➕ under the selection area of the Keyboard Shortcuts tab. Select an application from the Application pop-up menu. Type the menu command that you want to add and click in the Keyboard Shortcuts data field. Press the key combinations that you want for your shortcut and click **Add**.

What does the Use Two Fingers to Scroll option on the Trackpad tab do?

Clicking **Use two fingers to scroll** (changes to) under Trackpad Gestures enables more trackpad options when using a newer laptop. With your cursor in a scrollable window, you can now drag two fingers to scroll the window instead of having to click and drag the scrollbar. You can also check **Allow horizontal scrolling** for added flexibility.

When you start up a new Mac OS, you create an Administrator user account. This type of account enables you to access everything on the computer and install or update software. You can also add different user accounts with or without administrator privileges for others who use the computer, so they can have a separate Home folder and set their own preferences.

Create an Account

1 In System Preferences, click **Accounts**.

Note: *To view the System Preferences window, see the section "Change the Appearance of the Mac Interface" earlier in this chapter.*

The Accounts window opens.

Note: *You must be the administrator to create more accounts.*

2 Click the lock icon (🔒).

The Authenticate dialog box opens.

3 Type the password for the Administrator account.

4 Click **OK**.

The lock opens.

5 Click ⊞.

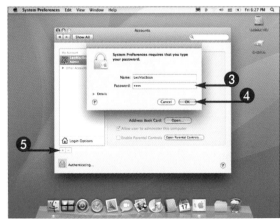

An Accounts dialog box appears.

6 In the data fields, type a new account name, the new account's password twice, and a password hint.

● Optionally, you can click ⬍ and select **Administrator** to allow administrator privileges.

7 Click **Create Account**.

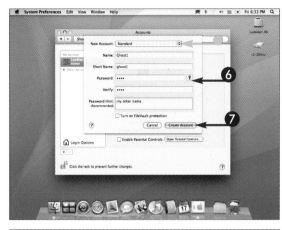

● The new account is created and listed under Other Accounts.

How do I change my password?

In the Accounts preference pane of System Preferences, click your account name. Click the **Password** tab and click **Change Password**. Type your current password in the Old Password field and a new password in the both the New Password and Verify fields and click **Change Password**.

I am the administrator, but I have forgotten my password. What do I do?

If you are already logged in, click your account name, click **Change Password**, and use the password hint to help you remember. If you cannot log in, you must reset the administrator password using the Mac OS X Install disc. Restart from the disc by holding down C when pressing the power key. Click **Installer** on the Installer menu and select **Reset Password**. Follow the onscreen steps to change your password.

Your Mac records the date and time of almost every operation that you perform. This feature enables you to search for specific items using the date and time, and you can determine which of two or more files with similar names is the most recent. Keeping the date and time set accurately helps organize your computer and your work.

Set the Date and Time

SET THE DATE AND TIME AUTOMATICALLY

Note: *This setting works best with an always-on Internet connection such as DSL or a cable modem.*

① In System Preferences, click **Date & Time**.

Note: *To view the System Preferences window, see the section "Change the Appearance of the Mac Interface" earlier in this chapter.*

The Date & Time window opens.

② Click **Date & Time**.

③ Click **Set date & time automatically** (☐ changes to ☑).

④ Click here and select the time server closest to you geographically.

The Mac sets the date and time using the Internet.

SET THE DATE AND TIME MANUALLY

① Click **Set date & time automatically** if it is checked (☑ changes to ☐).

② Click here and type the number for the current month.

③ Click here and type the current day.

④ Click here and type the current year.

Note: *You can also click the date calendar and click the arrows to advance the month and year.*

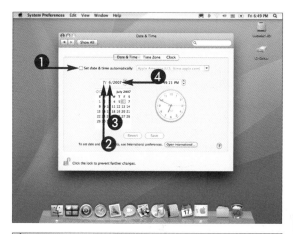

⑤ Click here and type the hour.

⑥ Click here and type the minute.

⑦ Click here and type **A** for AM or **P** for PM.

⑧ Click **Save**.

The date and time settings for the computer change.

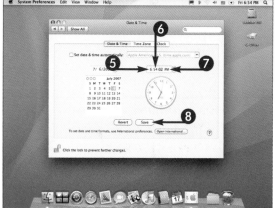

 TIP

How does my Mac know where I am to set the time automatically?

The Mac knows your location based on the time zone that you set when you first set up the computer. You can change the time zone using the Date & Time Preferences anytime, and the automatic time setting will reflect the current time at the new location. Click the **Time Zone** tab to see the world map. Click any location on the map, and the closest city to that location appears in the data field. You can also type the name of your city or use the ▾ to search for a city in the same time zone as your current location.

Customize the
Appearance of the Clock

You can set your Mac to display the time in the menu bar to make it always visible. You can also customize what the clock shows — for example, to include the seconds and the day of the week or to use a 24-hour format. You can even have the Mac announce the time at specified intervals. Customizing the clock's appearance is just another way Leopard gives you control over your Mac.

Customize the Appearance of the Clock

CHANGE THE CLOCK'S SETTINGS

① In System Preferences, click **Date & Time**.

Note: *To view the System Preferences window, see the section "Change the Appearance of the Mac Interface" earlier in this chapter.*

The Date & Time window opens.

② Click **Clock**.

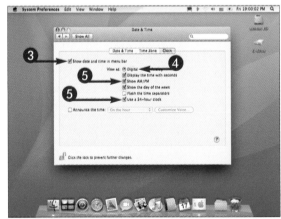

The Clock pane of the Date & Time window appears.

③ Click **Show date and time in menu bar** (☐ changes to ☑).

④ Click **Digital** (○ changes to ◉).

⑤ Click any of the check boxes listed to change the clock's appearance as you prefer (☐ changes to ☑).

Note: *Clicking **Analog** removes all these options.*

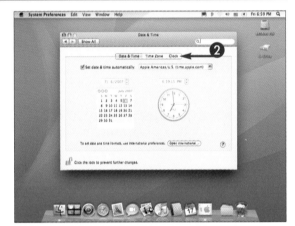

SET UP YOUR MAC TO ANNOUNCE THE TIME

6 Click **Announce the time** (☐ changes to ☑).

7 Click ⬍ to select the time interval.

8 Click **Customize Voice**.

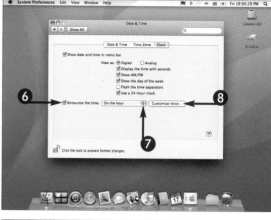

The Voice Preferences window opens.

9 Click ⬍ to select the voice.

10 Click **Play**.

The selected voice plays.

11 Click **Use custom volume** (☐ changes to ☑).

12 Click and drag the volume ▽.

13 Click **OK**.

Your clock settings take effect, and the time will now be announced as you have selected.

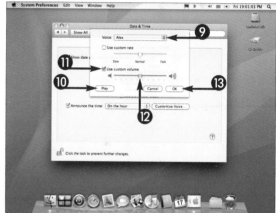

Can I move the clock display in the menu bar?

You can reposition the clock in the menu bar by pressing ⌘ and clicking and dragging the clock to a new location. The clock can only move to a different location on the right side of the menu bar.

Can I change the clock to a different country's language and convention?

You can switch to a 24-hour clock or readjust the way the clock displays the time to fit the conventions of another geographic area using the International Preferences window in System Preferences. Click **Formats** and then click **Show all regions** (☐ changes to ☑). Click ⬍ and select the geographic region from the list.

Update Your Software Automatically

Apple releases updates to its software anytime that there are important changes or fixes. There is no regular schedule for these updates; they are just part of the evolution and progress of the operating system. You can set up your Mac to automatically check and even download the updates in the background.

Update Your Software Automatically

① In System Preferences, click **Software Update**.

Note: To view the System Preferences window, see the section "Change the Appearance of the Mac Interface" earlier in this chapter.

The Software Update window opens.

② Click **Scheduled Check**.

③ Click **Check for updates** (☐ changes to ☑).

④ Click ⬍ and select a daily, weekly, or monthly time interval.

⑤ Click **Download important updates automatically** (☐ changes to ☑).

Any available updates will automatically be downloaded at the specified intervals.

⑥ Click **Check Now**.

● Your Mac checks the Apple update FTP server for new or updated system software, displaying the status of the check here.

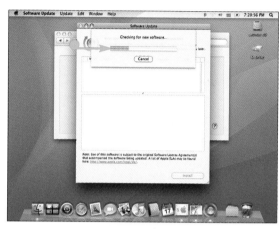

If there are updates, a window appears.

⑦ Click the software check boxes to select the items to install.

⑧ Click **Install** *number* **Items**.

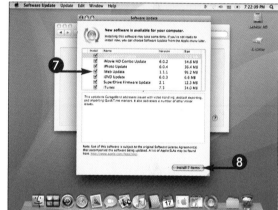

TIPS

Is there a faster way to check for software updates?

Instead of opening System Preferences, you can click in the menu bar and select **Software Update** directly.

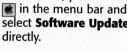

Does Software Update automatically install the updates?

No. Software Update only checks your system and compares it using the Internet to the database on Apple's servers. It only downloads updates automatically if that option is checked in the Preferences window. When Software Update finds a newer set of files, it asks you to confirm the download and installation before it proceeds with the updates.

Make Your Mac Speak

Leopard offers a new, more natural voice called *Alex*. You can set the Speech Preferences to read aloud any text that you highlight on the screen. You can also set your Mac to announce alerts when they are displayed and choose not only the voice for your Mac but also the rate of speech that it uses.

Make Your Mac Speak

SET THE ALEX VOICE'S SPEED

① In System Preferences, click **Speech**.

Note: To view the System Preferences window, see the section "Change the Appearance of the Mac Interface" earlier in this chapter.

The Speech Preferences pane opens.

② Click **Text to Speech**.

The Speech Preferences window changes.

③ Click 🔽 and select **Alex**.

④ Click **Play**.

The computer recites a demonstration sentence in the Alex voice.

⑤ Click and drag 🔘, to the right for faster speech or to the left for slower speech.

⑥ Click **Play**.

The computer recites the same phrase more quickly or more slowly.

⑦ Repeat steps **5** to **6** until the speech is the speed that you prefer.

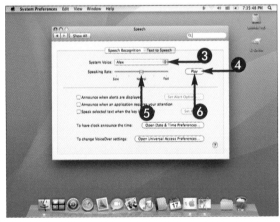

HAVE ALERTS ANNOUNCED

⑧ Click **Announce when alerts are displayed** (changes to ☑).

You Mac will now read aloud any alerts that appear onscreen.

⑨ Click **Set Alert Options**.

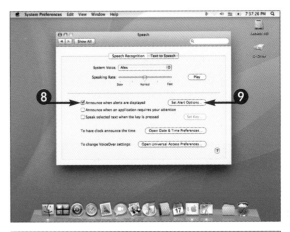

The Voice Selection Preferences open.

⑩ Click this ⬍ and select **Alex**.

⑪ Click this ⬍ and select **Attention!**

⑫ Click and drag ◎ to 10 seconds.

⑬ Click **OK**.

You Mac will now wait 10 seconds before it says "Attention" and reads aloud any alerts.

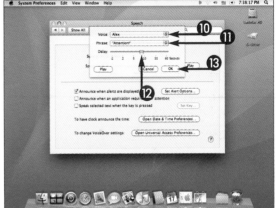

TIPS

Why is Announce When an Application Requires Your Attention a separate selection in the Speech Preferences window?

An application sometimes requires your input to continue with a task, but its request for your attention is not technically an alert. With this option checked, the Mac will notify you verbally rather than let you continue typing, for example, only to find that nothing was entered.

How do I make the Mac speak some text?

On the Text to Speech tab of the Speech Preferences, click **Speak selected text when the key is pressed** (changes to ☑). Click **Set Key**. Type modifier keys and another key, such as ⌘ + Shift + T, and click **OK**. Select some text in any window and press these keys. The voice reads the text aloud. Press the keys again to have the voice stop reading.

"I'll speak in a monstrous little voice."
A Midsummer Night's Dream

Control Your Mac with Voice Commands

You can train your Mac to respond to certain voice commands. For example, you can make your Mac automatically open or close a window or empty the Trash by selecting these commands in the Speech Preferences. You can also control when the computer should listen for a verbal command.

Control Your Mac with Voice Commands

① In System Preferences, click **Speech**.

Note: *To view the System Preferences window, see the section "Change the Appearance of the Mac Interface" earlier in this chapter.*

The Speech Preferences pane opens.

② Click **Speech Recognition**.

③ Click **On** (○ changes to ⊙).

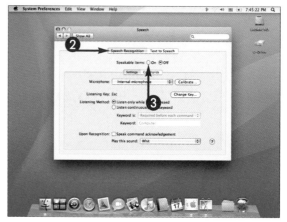

● A Speech Recognition icon appears on the desktop indicating audio level.

④ Click **Settings**.

⑤ Click **Listen continuously with keyword** (○ changes to ⊙).

⑥ Type a keyword such as **Computer** here.

Note: You can type any keyword that you want in the field.

⑦ Click **Commands**.

The Speech Preferences window changes.

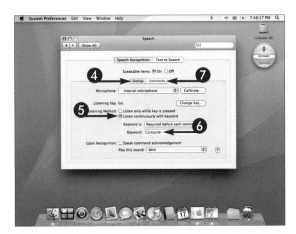

⑧ Click **Menu Bar** or another area for which you want to activate voice commands (□ changes to ☑).

⑨ First say your keyword and then one of the preset voice commands – for example, "Computer, what time is it?"

● The computer uses the selected voice to respond – for example, to state the time and briefly displays the question and answer.

How do I know what commands I can use?

Click the **Open Speakable Items Folder** button on the Commands tab of the Speech Recognition pane. The Speakable Items window appears, showing a list of general speakable commands. Double-click the **Application Speakable Items** folder to see a list of the application-specific commands that you can use.

How can I improve my Mac's speech recognition?

Your microphone dictates the quality of the voice recognition. You can select the microphone that you are using in the Speech Preferences window. Click **Calibrate**. Speak continuously while moving the slider until the meter stays in the green area. Test each phrase listed on the left. The text blinks when it is recognized. Move the slider more if necessary.

Control the Zoom and Contrast of Your Screen

Although the Universal Access pane in the System Preferences is intended to help people with hearing, vision, or mobility difficulties, some of the options are useful for every Mac user. If you turn on the Zoom option, you can zoom in to better see an image in any application. You can also use the slider to increase the contrast on your screen.

Control the Zoom and Contrast of Your Screen

① In System Preferences, click **Universal Access**.

Note: To view the System Preferences window, see the section "Change the Appearance of the Mac Interface" earlier in this chapter.

The Universal Access Preferences appear.

② Click **Seeing**.

③ Click **On** under Zoom (⚪ changes to ⦿).

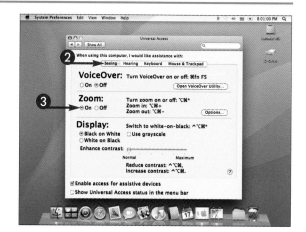

④ Press ⌘+Option+═.

The screen zooms in.

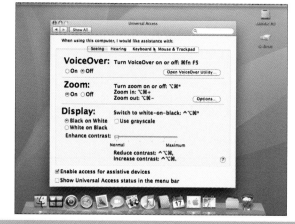

⑤ Press ⌘ + **Option** + **=** again.

The screen zooms in more.

⑥ Press ⌘ + **Option** + **-** twice.

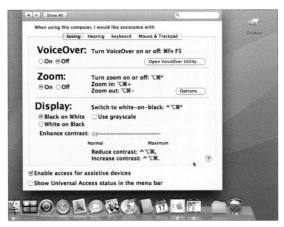

The screen zooms out to its original size.

⑦ In the Display section, click and drag the ⊡ to the right.

The display contrast of black on white increases.

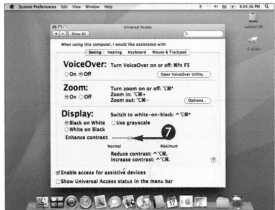

 TIPS

What other Universal Access Preferences may be useful to the average user?

Depending on the screen resolution and application, the cursor can sometimes be difficult to see. You can increase the cursor size by clicking the **Mouse & Trackpad** tab of the Universal Access Preferences and then clicking and dragging the Cursor Size slider. The cursor enlarges.

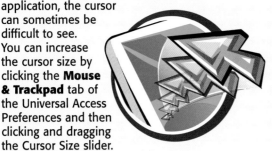

What is the screen flash for under the Hearing Preferences pane?

Clicking **Flash the screen when an alert sound occurs** helps people with hearing difficulties. This option is also useful when working in a library or other quiet environment. If you click **Adjust Volume** and then click **Mute** (☐ changes to ☑) by the Output volume, the Mac alerts you without the usual beep or other sounds.

Using Leopard Applications for Everyday Tasks

Mac OS X Leopard is system software designed to make your Mac function at the basic level. Unlike other types of system software, however, Mac OS X includes many built-in applications that make a variety of frequent tasks easy and quick to accomplish. This chapter describes how to use some of these bundled applications.

Find Items on Your Computer with Spotlight

Even if you are very organized with your files and folders, you probably spend time every day finding items on your computer. Spotlight is a searching application that can find anything on your Mac as well as on other remote Macs or volumes on the network. Leopard's version of Spotlight also enables you to open found files and launch the application directly from the Spotlight window.

Find Items on Your Computer with Spotlight

SEARCH WITH THE SPOTLIGHT ICON

① Click the Spotlight icon (🔍).

A search box appears.

② Type a word or phrase indicating what you are searching for.

Spotlight displays a search results list as you type, with the results grouped by type.

③ Click the file that you want in the list.

Spotlight automatically launches the application or displays the file in Preview.

SEARCH IN A FINDER WINDOW

1 Click [icon] in the Dock.

The Finder window opens.

2 Click in the Spotlight search box.

3 Type a word or a phrase indicating what you are searching for.

● Spotlight displays a search results window as you type, with the results grouped by type.

4 Click an item to select it.

● Spotlight reveals the hierarchical path to the file at the bottom of the window.

TIPS

Does Spotlight search only by filename?

Spotlight searches filenames as well as other information within files. For example, music files in iTunes contain information such as the artist, album, and musical genre. Digital photo files contain information about the camera model, image size, date taken, and more. You can thus search your photos for all the ones taken with a particular camera or on a particular date.

Can I limit my search to exclude certain items?

Leopard's Spotlight is more powerful than the previous version. It uses Boolean logic to narrow search results. When you enter **AND**, **OR**, or **NOT** in the search field, you can refine your Spotlight search. For example, if you type **"smith"** **AND "jane"** in your Address Book search field, Spotlight will show only Jane Smith and not John Smith.

Mac OS X Leopard includes an application to quickly preview specific files, photos, and more. With Preview, you can quickly view and print various types of files or check the details of any document without launching the associated application. Preview is perfect for quickly viewing photos and other graphic files, as well as checking text documents including multipage PDFs.

① In the Finder, click **Go**.

② Click **Applications**.

● You can also click the Preview icon if it is in your Dock.

A Finder window opens listing the contents of the Applications folder.

③ Press P in any Finder view mode to automatically scroll down to applications starting with the letter *P* in the list.

④ Press Tab to move to the next application starting with the letter P.

⑤ Repeat step **4** if necessary.

⑥ Double-click **Preview**.

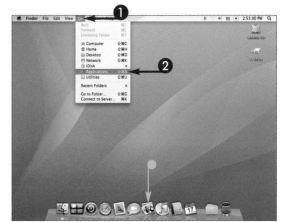

The Preview application launches.

7 Click **File**.

8 Click **Open**.

The Open dialog box appears.

9 Click a file to select it.

10 Click **Open**.

Preview opens the file.

 TIPS

I opened a multipage PDF, but I only see one page. How can I see the other pages?

Click the Sidebar icon (⬚) in the Preview window. The sidebar opens, displaying thumbnails of all the pages in the document.

Can I use the Preview application to change the filename and file formats?

You can easily change filenames and formats with Preview. With the file open, click **File → Save As**. In the dialog box that appears, type a new name for the file and click the Format ⬚ to select the new file format. Click **Save**.

Personalize the Preview Application

Preview is a very powerful application. Not only can you view image files and read PDFs and other documents without launching specific applications, but you can also select areas, rotate and crop images, annotate files, and check the file's metadata. Personalizing Preview's toolbar makes all these tasks quick and easy.

Personalize the Preview Application

① With any file open in the Preview application, click **View**.

② Click **Customize Toolbar**.

The toolbar items dialog box appears.

③ Click and drag the items that you want to the toolbar.

● Try adding the Rotate, Inspector, and Print tools to the toolbar.

Note: *You can place these wherever you want on the toolbar.*

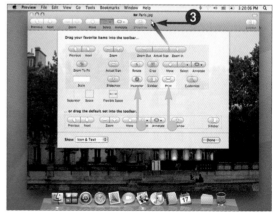

The toolbar immediately displays the added tool icons.

4 Click **Done**.

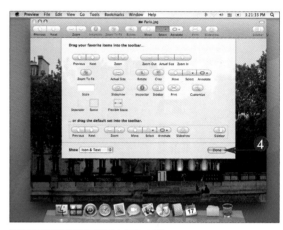

The toolbar items window closes.

5 Click one of the new tools that you added, such as **Inspector** .

In this example, the Inspector tool displays the file information in a separate window.

TIPS

How can I revert to the original Preview toolbar?

With the toolbar items dialog box open, you can remove any individual tool icon by clicking and dragging it off the toolbar. You can also revert to the original toolbar by clicking and dragging the default set into the current toolbar. The default set immediately replaces the current toolbar.

What is the Bookmarks menu item for?

With a multipage document, you may want to bookmark a specific page so that you can return to it quickly. To add a bookmark, click **Bookmarks** → **Add Bookmark**. Type a name for the bookmark in the data field and click **Add**. The bookmarked item or page is now listed under the **Preview Bookmarks** menu for quick reference.

Add a Contact to the Address Book

The Address Book included with Mac OS X Leopard enables you to store and look up information for friends or business contacts and stay organized using the same information with other applications, such as Apple's Mail program and Safari. You can easily build a complete directory of names and addresses to make mailing and networking more efficient.

Add a Contact to the Address Book

ADD A CONTACT

1. In the Dock, click the Address Book icon (![icon]).

   The Address Book application launches.

2. Click **All** in the Group column.

3. Under the Name column, click ⊞.

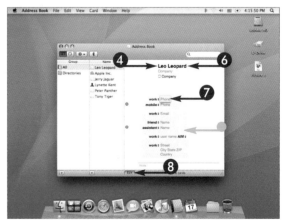

A new blank contact card is created.

4. Type a first name in the First field.

5. Press Tab to move to the next field.

6. Type a last name in the Last field.

7. Click the **Phone** field and type a phone number.

   ● You can enter as much information into the other fields as you have.

8. Click **Edit**.

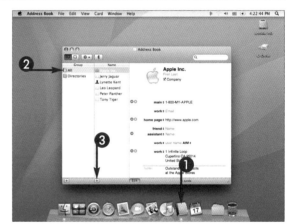

The name and contact information are added to the card, and the card is listed in the Name column.

EDIT A CONTACT

9 Click the contact to edit in the Name column.

The contact card appears.

10 Click **Edit**.

11 Click any data field and type in the new information.

12 Click **Edit**.

The contact is updated in the Address Book according to your changes.

TIPS

Should I fill out a contact card for myself?

A card with a figure in the list is already started for you as the Mac user. You can add your address, phone numbers, and more to fill out the Me card, creating a virtual business card that you can send to others. The Safari Web browser can also use this information to automatically fill out forms on Web pages for you.

Me
322 W. Main St.
555-555-4657

What else can the Address Book do to help me save time?

The Address Book can automatically launch Safari and show you a map of the address that you select. With a contact card open, click the Action button (⚙▾) and click **Map This Address** from the drop-down menu. Safari launches and links to Google Maps for the selected address.

Mark A. David
2211 W. 9th St.
555-885-4657

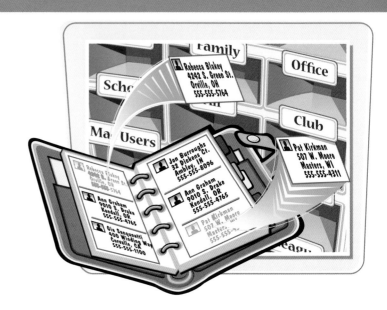

You can put contact cards into different groups to better organize your Address Book. You can even put the same card into different groups so that you can organize your addresses in multiple ways. Also, the Address Book enables you to send an email to all the members of a group with one click.

Organize Your Contacts

CREATE A GROUP

① In the Address Book, click [+] under the Group column.

② Type a name for the new group.

③ Press [Return].

ADD A CONTACT TO THE GROUP

① Click **All**.

The Address Book displays all your contacts.

② Click and drag a contact to the new group.

REMOVE A CONTACT FROM A GROUP

1 In the Name column, click the name of the contact that you want to remove.

2 Click **Edit**.

3 Click **Remove From Group**.

The contact card is removed from the group but not from the Address Book.

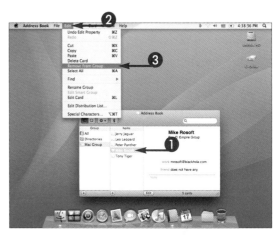

SEND AN EMAIL TO A GROUP

1 Press **Ctrl** and click the name of a group in the Group column.

2 Click **Send Email to "Group Name"**.

The Mail application launches and opens a new email with the email addresses for each contact in the group.

3 Type and send your email.

Note: To learn more about using email, see Chapter 6.

TIPS

If I delete a group, are all the contacts removed from my Address Book?

No. Whether you delete an entire group or remove a contact from a group, the contacts remain in your Address Book. To remove a contact from your Address Book, click the contact name under the All group. Click **Edit → Delete Card**.

Can I add a picture to a contact's card?

Yes. First, click the contact. Click **Card → Choose Custom Image**. In the photo window that appears, click **Choose** and navigate to a photo file on your computer to use for the contact. Click **Open**, and the photo is placed in the photo window. Click **Set**, and the photo is added to the contact in the Address Book.

Find an Address on a Map

Mac OS Leopard's Address Book application can do much more than help you store and organize your addresses. With an Internet connection, you can use the Address Book to locate any address on a map.

321 W. Atley St.
Paris, Illinois 65321

Find an Address on a Map

1 Click  in the Dock.

The Address Book opens.

2 Click **All**.

Note: You can also click a group if your group names contain addresses.

3 Click the name of the contact whose address you want to see on a map in the Name column.

4 Click the address label.

A pop-up menu appears.

⑤ Click **Map Of**.

The Address Book opens the Safari browser and displays a map of the location.

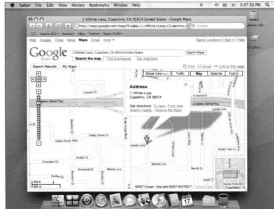

TIPS

What else can I do with the Address Book?

You can use the Address Book to print address books, mailing labels, and envelopes. You can also use it to keep track of birthdays, send change of address notifications to your contacts, and find contacts quickly with a Spotlight search.

How do I print an Address Book?

Press ⌘ and click the contacts to print. Click **File → Print**. Click the Show More button (▾) to expand the Print dialog box. Click **Style** and select **Pocket Address Book**. Click the items that you want to include in Attributes. Select the **Flip Style**, click **Set** to select a different font, and click **Print**.

Using the Calculator

The Mac OS, like most traditional office desktops, includes a calculator. Leopard's calculator is actually very sophisticated and powerful. Not only can it perform basic calculations, but it can also transform into a scientific calculator and even a programmer's calculator. You can use the calculator to quickly convert weights, temperatures, and more.

Using the Calculator

USING THE BASIC CALCULATOR

1 Press ⌘ + Shift + A to open the Applications folder.

2 Double-click **Calculator**.

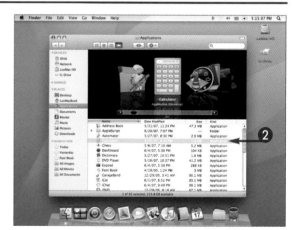

The basic calculator appears on the desktop.

You can close the Applications window.

3 Click the number and function keys to perform the math that you need.

4 Click the = key.

● The result of your calculation appears here.

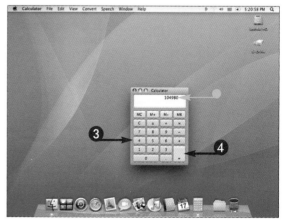

CONVERT FAHRENHEIT TO CELSIUS

① Type the current temperature in Fahrenheit degrees.

② Click **Convert**.

③ Click **Temperature**.

The temperature conversion dialog box appears.

④ Click the From ◆ and select **Fahrenheit**.

⑤ Click the To ◆ and select **Celsius**.

⑥ Click **OK**.

● The calculator displays the temperature in degrees Celsius.

Note: You can also convert Celsius to Fahrenheit. Other unit conversions on the Convert menu can be done the same way.

USING THE SCIENTIFIC CALCULATOR

① Click **View**.

② Click **Scientific**.

The calculator changes to a horizontal display with scientific functions.

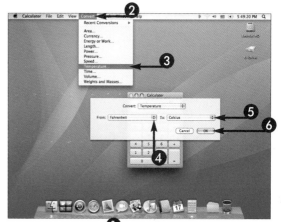

TIPS

Can I set the calculator to round the results instead of showing so many decimal places?

Yes. You can specify the number of decimal places to display and round the results of any calculations. Click **View → Decimal Places**. Then click the number of decimal places that you prefer.

What is the Show Paper Tape option for on the Window menu?

Clicking **Show Paper Tape** enables you to see the calculations as they are entered and print them as you would with a manual calculator with a paper tape. The Print function is listed under the File menu.

Mac OS X Leopard includes a calendar application called *iCal* to help you stay organized with appointments and to-do lists. You can lay out different types of calendars and customize them for different purposes. iCal enables you to create multiple calendars such as one for home projects and another for work and color-code them differently for quick viewing.

Track Your Schedule

CREATE A NEW CALENDAR

① Click the iCal icon (⊞) in the Dock.

The iCal application launches.

② Click +.

A new unnamed calendar appears in the Calendars list.

③ Type a name for the new calendar.

④ Press Return.

⑤ Press ⌘+I.

An info page opens with the new group name, a description field, and a color option box.

⑥ Click here to select a different color for the group calendar.

*Note: Clicking **Other** opens the Color Picker to choose a new color.*

⑦ Click OK.

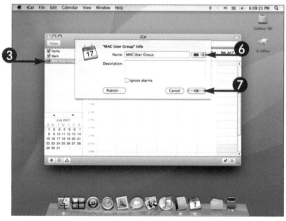

ADD AN EVENT TO A CALENDAR

① Click the calendar in the Calendars list.

② Click **Month**.

③ Click ◄ or ► to select the month.

The calendar displays the selected month.

④ Double-click the day for the event.

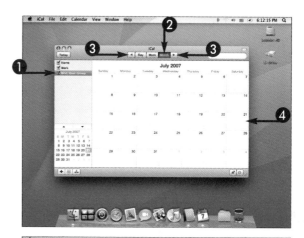

A new event field appears in the calendar.

⑤ Type the name of the new event.

⑥ Press Return.

⑦ Double-click the event on the Calendar.

A details page appears.

⑧ Click any data field to add information such as time and location.

⑨ Click Done.

The details page disappears, leaving only the name of the event on the calendar.

 TIPS

How do I remove an event from a calendar?

Click the event that you want to remove and press Delete or click **Edit** in the menu and click **Delete**.

Can I schedule blocks of time?

You can assign blocks of time to any event when the calendar displays either the day or week. Click either the **Day** or **Week** buttons at the top of the calendar. Click the event and then click and drag the bottom of the event's colored block down until the end time is reached.

Subscribe to a Calendar

The Internet offers many free calendars, including official holidays in different countries, sporting events, and other important dates. By subscribing to one or more of these online calendars, you can quickly include the special dates in your own personal calendars.

Subscribe to a Calendar

① In iCal, click **Calendar**.

② Click **Subscribe**.

The Subscribe data field appears.

③ Type the address of the calendar to which you want to subscribe, such as **webcal://ical.mac.com/ical/US32Holidays.ics**.

④ Click **Subscribe**.

⑤ Click **OK** in the confirmation dialog box that appears.

The new calendar appears in the Calendars list, and the events from the subscribed calendar are highlighted in a matching color.

6 Click the new calendar in the list.

7 Click **Month**.

8 Click ◄ or ► to select the month.

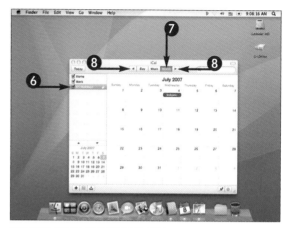

iCal displays the events for that month on the calendar — the U.S. holidays in this example.

How do I cancel a calendar subscription?

You can cancel a subscription by deleting the specific calendar from the list. Click the calendar name in the Calendars list and press Delete , or click **Edit** in the menu and click **Delete**.

Where can I find other calendars that I can select from?

You can find many other specialized calendars on the Web. Open a Web browser such as Safari and type **http://icalshare.com** or **www.apple.com/macosx/features/ical/library** to find many other subscription calendars.

iCal is more than a series of separate calendars to help you stay organized. Using a service such as .Mac, you can publish or share your calendar so that people in your organization can stay current. You can also set up a special event and use iCal to help you automatically send email invitations to friends and family.

Using iCal to Manage Your Work and Home Life

PUBLISH A CALENDAR

1 In iCal, click a calendar to publish.

2 Click **Calendar**.

3 Click **Publish**.

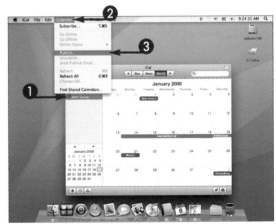

The iCal Publish dialog box appears.

4 Type a name for the calendar.

5 Click the Publish On 🔹 and select **.Mac** or a private server.

Note: To learn more about .Mac, see Chapter 10.

6 Click **Publish**.

iCal publishes the calendar on your .Mac account and gives you a URL for members of your organization to access it.

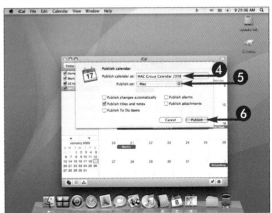

SEND EVENT INVITATIONS

1 In iCal, create an event.

Note: To create an event, see "Track Your Schedule" earlier in this chapter.

2 Double-click the event to view the details.

3 Click **Window**.

4 Click **Address Panel**.

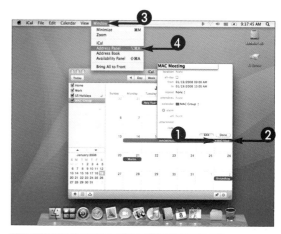

An Addresses window from your Address Book opens.

5 Click and drag the names of the people to invite to the event details drawer.

● iCal lists the people under **attendees**.

6 Click **Send**.

The Mail application launches, and an email opens, ready for you to design and send.

TIPS

How do I update a published calendar or remove it?

To make sure that the published calendar updates when you change items, click **Calendar → Refresh**. iCal will send the information and update the published calendar. To remove a calendar, click **Calendar → Unpublish**. The calendar is automatically removed from the site.

How can I keep track of birthdays?

First list the birthdays in the Address Book cards. Click **All** (or any group) and click **Card → Add Field → Birthday** in the Address Book menu. Fill out the birthdays on the Address Book cards. In iCal, click **iCal → Preferences**. Under **General**, click **Show Birthdays calendar**. Any listed birthdays will now appear on the calendar.

Write and Style a Document with TextEdit

Mac OS X Leopard includes a simple-to-use, yet powerful word-processor application called *TextEdit*. You can type letters, create a variety of documents, format the documents with different font styles, and even add active Weblinks. TextEdit can not only read but can also save documents in all the most commonly used formats.

Write and Style a Document with TextEdit

TYPE AND ADD A STYLE TO TEXT

1. Press ⌘ + Shift + A to open the Applications folder.

2. Press Option and double-click **TextEdit**.

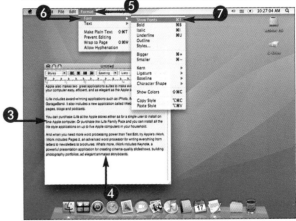

TextEdit launches and opens an untitled document, and the Applications windows closes.

3. Type your text.

4. Click and drag across the text to add a style.

Note: You can press ⌘ + A to select all the text.

5. Click **Format**.

6. Click **Font**.

7. Click **Show Fonts**.

The Font dialog box appears.

⑧ Click a font family name.

⑨ Click a typeface.

⑩ Click a size.

The selected text in the untitled document interactively changes with the selections.

⑪ Click the green Text color box.

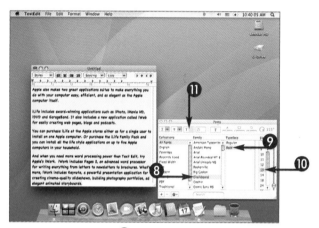

The Colors dialog box appears.

⑫ Click and drag the color slider to the top.

The brightest colors appear in the color wheel.

⑬ Click in the color wheel to select another color.

The text color changes.

⑭ Click .

The Colors dialog box closes.

⑮ Click .

The Font dialog box closes.

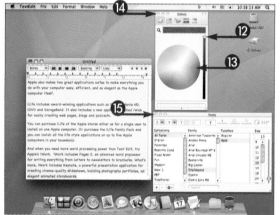

TIPS

Can TextEdit check my spelling as I write?

You can check the spelling of a document by clicking **Edit → Spelling and Grammar → Check Spelling and Grammar**. You can also make TextEdit automatically check the spelling and underline misspelled words in red as you type. Click **Edit → Spelling and Grammar → Check Spelling While Typing**.

How can I save a text style for later use?

Format some text using the font, font style, color, and more as shown here. Click the Styles ▼ in the TextEdit window and click **Other**. Click **Add To Favorites** in the Styles dialog box that appears. **Add To Favorites** is also found in the menu, by clicking **Format → Font → Styles**.

continued ➤

Because you can save TextEdit documents in a variety of formats, the TextEdit files that you create can be read by most other word-processing applications. And because TextEdit can read all sorts of file formats, you can open and read almost any text document that you receive, including HTML and Microsoft Word files.

CREATE A WEBLINK

① Click and drag across some text to link.

② Click **Format**.

③ Click **Text**.

④ Click **Link**.

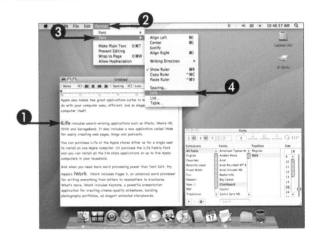

A dialog box appears.

⑤ Type the Internet address including the suffix such as .com or .net in the Link Destination field.

⑥ Click **OK**.

The text is underlined and an interactive Weblink is created.

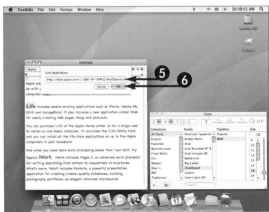

SAVE THE TEXT FILE

1 Click **File**.

2 Click **Save As**.

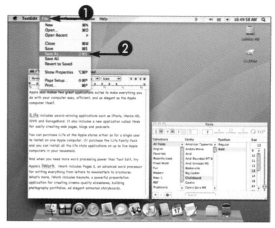

The Save As dialog box appears.

3 Type a name into the Save As data field.

4 Click here and navigate to a folder in which to save the file.

5 Click the File Format and select the format in which you want to save, such as **Rich Text Format (RTF)**.

6 Click **Save**.

The document is saved with the style and the interactive Weblink.

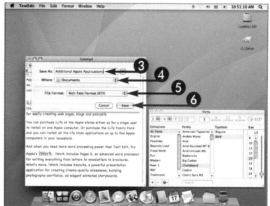

 TIPS

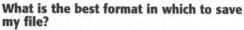

Can I include photos in a TextEdit document?

You can place not only photos but also movies in a TextEdit file by dragging the photo or movie into the document window. Only documents saved in RTF and Word formats can include graphics. The photo or movie will appear as an embedded graphic alongside the text.

What is the best format in which to save my file?

TextEdit can view and edit a number of different file formats. Because most word processors, including Microsoft Word, can open rich text format (RTF) files, this is generally a good choice. RTF files can include embedded graphics and preserve text styles. You can use the other formats when you know what application will be used to open the file.

Consult the Dictionary

Mac OS X Leopard includes not only a built-in dictionary but also a thesaurus. You can even view a word in both references at the same time. The dictionary application is interactive, so you can double-click any word in the dictionary that you want clarified, and that word then appears in the dictionary and thesaurus with its description.

Consult the Dictionary

1 Press ⌘ + Shift + A to open the Applications folder.

2 Press Option and double-click **Dictionary**.

The Dictionary window appears, and the Applications window closes.

3 Type a word in the Spotlight data field in the window.

As you type, the found entries appear in a list.

4 Double-click an entry for your word.

The dictionary displays the word definition.

⑤ Click **Thesaurus**.

The synonyms for the word appear.

⑥ Click the Increase Font Size button (Ⓐ).

The entry becomes larger and easier to read.

⑦ Move the cursor over a synonym.

The word appears highlighted and underlined, indicating that it is a link.

● You can click the word to view it in the dictionary.

Is there a quick way to look up a word when I am writing in TextEdit?

You can use a shortcut to the dictionary when you are using certain applications, including TextEdit and Safari. Highlight the word and press Ctrl while clicking the mouse. Select **Look Up in Dictionary** from the contextual menu that appears. For a faster shortcut, place the cursor in the word. Then press ⌘+Ctrl+D. A small dictionary panel opens with a definition. Click **More** on the panel to launch the dictionary application and see the complete listing for the word.

A *screenshot* is a picture of what is displayed on your monitor. Screenshots are useful for capturing a window for future reference. A screenshot can often help tech support troubleshoot a problem for you. You can capture the full screen, a part of the screen, a window, or a specific menu using the included Grab application.

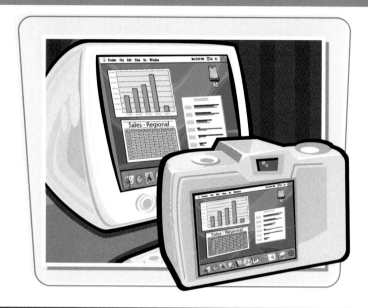

Capture a Screenshot

① With the display that you want to capture up, click the desktop to return to the Finder.

② Press ⌘ + Shift + U to open the Utilities folder.

③ Press Option and double-click **Grab**.

The Grab application launches, and the Utilities window closes.

④ Click **Capture**.

⑤ Click **Screen**.

The Screen grab explanation dialog box appears.

6 Click the mouse pointer anywhere outside the Screen Grab dialog box.

Grab makes a camera-click noise, captures the screenshot, and displays it.

7 Click **File**.

8 Click **Save**.

9 Type a name in the Save As dialog box that appears.

10 Click here and select a location to save the file.

11 Click **Save**.

The file is saved as a .tiff file in the location that you selected.

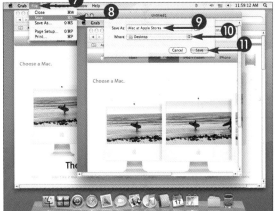

 TIPS

What does the Timed Screen option on the Capture menu do?

When you click **Capture →
Timed Screen** in the Grab menu, you tell Grab to take the screenshot ten seconds after you click **Start Timer** in the Timed Screen Grab window. This is useful when you need to open a menu before taking a screenshot.

Can I take a screenshot without launching the Grab application?

Yes. You can grab a screenshot almost anytime by pressing ⌘+Shift+3. The Mac makes a camera shutter sound and places a PNG image file on the desktop. Also, you can press ⌘+Shift+4 to change the cursor into a crosshair pointer and then click and drag over an area and release the mouse button. The area is captured, and the PNG file appears on the desktop.

Keep Your Projects Organized with Spaces

Mac OS X Leopard includes a new tool for keeping you organized, no matter how many different projects you work on. Spaces is a new bundled application that enables you to group all your open documents and running applications into separate project areas.

Multiple Project Studios

Using Spaces is like having a suite of different work studios, each equipped with tools for a different project. In System Preferences, you can build up to 16 separate spaces and keep all the applications and files that you need for each project ready in each studio.

Remodel Your Spaces

You not only determine what is available in each space but also decide where each space resides on the grid, moving the individual spaces around as you would when remodeling the layout in a real studio. All you have to do in Spaces is click and drag them to a new grid square.

Move from Space to Space

You can get an overall view of all the spaces at once by pressing the keyboard shortcut F8. Then click directly on the space that you want to work in. The open applications and files for that project appear on your desktop with no other open windows to distract you.

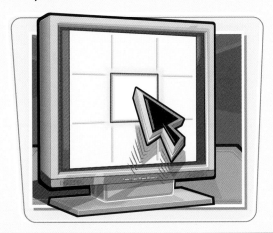

Applications and Spaces

You can assign applications to each space, and an application can be included in all the spaces. For example, you may use iCal in your office space along with TextEdit, the calculator, and various open text documents. You may also use iCal in your home or family space, along with iChat, Mail, and a photo-editing application such as iPhoto.

Toggle around Your Spaces

You can move around your spaces using the default keys (Ctrl and the arrow keys), or you can go directly to the number of the space that you want to work in by pressing Ctrl and the number key for that space. Spaces clears off your desktop and displays only that space's open files and applications.

Space Docking

The Dock acts like a central command post for your spaces by showing the open applications. With Spaces active, clicking an application in the Dock takes you directly to a space that includes that application.

Customize Your Personal Space

Mac OS X Leopard enables you to set up your space or spaces the way you like for work and play. You can set up the number of different workspaces, rearrange them in any order, assign specific applications to each space, and set up the keyboard shortcuts that you want to use to go from space to space.

Customize Your Personal Space

① In the System Preferences window, click **Exposé & Spaces**.

The Exposé & Spaces Preferences appear.

② Click **Spaces**.

③ Click **Enable Spaces** (☐ changes to ☑).

④ Click the Rows ⊕.

⑤ Click the Columns ⊕.

⑥ Repeat steps **4** to **5** until you have the number of rows and columns that you want.

Note: *You can have as few as 2 and as many as 16 separate spaces.*

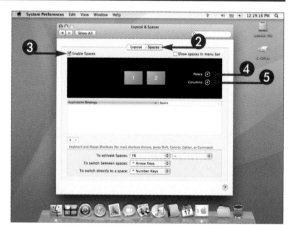

⑦ Click ☐+☐.

An Applications pane appears.

⑧ Click an application and click **Add**.

⑨ Repeat steps **7** to **8** to add other applications.

● Optionally, you can press ⌘+click any number of applications to add them all at once.

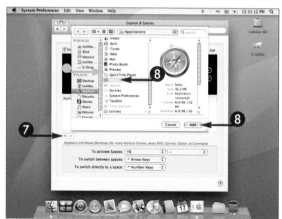

The added applications appear in the window.

⑩ Click the Space ⬍ in line with an application that you want to change to a different Space.

⑪ Click **Space number**.

⑫ Repeat steps **10** to **11** for each application, changing the assigned space number.

Note: *Set up each space with the applications that you need for a project.*

⑬ Click ⊙ to close System Preferences.

⑭ Press F8.

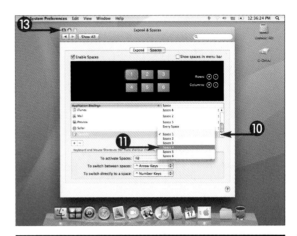

The spaces all appear at once on a grid.

⑮ Click any space to go to that work area.

What is the difference between Exposé and Spaces?

Exposé enables you to temporarily arrange your open windows and desktop and helps you find things. With Exposé, you can see all open windows at once, only the windows for one application, or a clear desktop. Spaces helps you work on an uncluttered desktop by keeping open and available only those applications and files included in the project's space.

Do I have to set up different keyboard shortcuts?

No. You can use the default keyboard shortcuts such as F8 to see the spaces and Ctrl + the arrow keys to move around. To access a specific project's space, click the project's open application in the Dock, and that space opens. If, however, the application is included in all the spaces, the application comes to the front, but the space does not change.

Harnessing the Power of the Internet

The Internet opens the world on your desktop. Exploring all the Internet has to offer, from an abundance of information to basic communication through email, can be complex. Mac OS X Leopard includes simple yet powerful tools to help you surf the Web, send and receive emails, and read news feeds.

Safari is the Web browser from Apple that comes built in with Mac OS X Leopard. You can use other browsers with Leopard; however, Safari offers many advantages, including the speed with which it loads Web pages and the SnapBack option. You can view pages without typing the full URL and return to a previously visited page with one click.

Surf the Web with Safari

① In the Dock, click the Safari icon (⬡).

The Safari Web browser launches and displays the default Apple page.

② Click here and drag to highlight the entire Web address.

③ Type the name and suffix of the Web site that you want to visit, such as **wiley.com**.

④ Press Return.

Safari automatically fills in the rest of the required URL address and loads the page.

*Note: You can type most Web pages using just the name and the appropriate suffix such as .com without first typing **http://www**.*

⑤ Press ⬇.

The page scrolls down in steps.

⑥ Press ⬆.

The page scrolls up in steps.

⑦ Press Spacebar.

The page jumps down to the next section of the page.

⑧ Press Shift + Spacebar.

The page jumps up to the previous section of the page.

⑨ Click a link of interest.

Safari loads the page associated with the link.

⑩ Click the SnapBack button (⬅).

The page snaps back to your most recent results page –
in this example, the main Wiley publishing page.

 TIPS

How do I open a link in a new window?

Press Ctrl and click a link. Select **Open Link in New Window** from the menu that appears. Although you can use keyboard shortcuts for opening links in different ways, the shortcuts differ depending on your selections in the Tabs section of the Safari Preferences. See the section "Using Tabbed Browsing" for more information about tabs in Safari.

Is there a quick way to delete a URL in the address before I retype a new one?

Pressing ⌘ + L highlights the address in the address section of the toolbar. Type in the new URL and press Return. Remember with Safari that you only have to type the name and the suffix, such as **apple.com**, not the entire URL.

Block Pop-up Windows

Pop-up windows are generally unwanted advertisements that appear when you open or close a Web page. They can clutter your screen and sometimes slow your browser down or make it unresponsive. You can block pop-up windows in Safari to avoid this.

Block Pop-up Windows

BLOCK POP-UP WINDOWS USING THE SAFARI MENU

❶ In the Safari menu bar, click **Safari**.

❷ Click **Block Pop-Up Windows**.

Safari prevents most pop-up windows from opening.

Note: *Pop-up windows may still appear when you click a link on a Web page.*

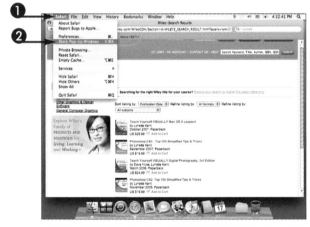

BLOCK POP-UP WINDOWS USING A KEYSTROKE

❶ In Safari, press ⌘+Shift+K.

Note: *The keystroke toggles pop-up windows on and off.*

● If you open the Safari menu, you will see that the option Block Pop-Up Windows is checked.

Google is one of the largest search engines on the Internet. Safari includes a built-in Google search field in the Address bar so that you can start a search without having to change Web pages. Safari also includes a SnapBack button in the Google search field as well as a Review button to see all your recent searches.

Search Using Google

1 In Safari, click in the Google search field and type a word or phrase.

2 Press `Return`.

Safari queries Google and displays the search results.

3 Click in the Google search field and type another word or phrase.

4 Press `Return`.

Safari displays the new search results.

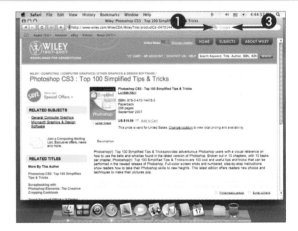

5 Click the Recent Search button (🔍▾).

A drop-down menu opens, displaying previous Google searches.

6 Click a recent search in the list.

Safari displays the previous Google search page.

Organize Web Sites with Bookmarks

Mac OS X Leopard helps you stay organized even when you surf the Web. Using Safari, you can bookmark your often-visited Web pages for quick access later on. You can group your bookmarks into different collections and make your favorites readily available by keeping them in the Bookmarks bar.

Organize Web Sites with Bookmarks

ADD A BOOKMARK

1 In Safari, navigate to a favorite Web page.

2 Click **Bookmarks**.

3 Click **Add Bookmark**.

● You can add a new folder to the list of Bookmark folders by clicking **Add Bookmark Folder** and typing a name for the new folder.

A dialog box opens.

4 Type a name for the bookmark in the highlighted field.

5 Click the Bookmarks Bar 🔽.

A list of bookmark folders and locations appears.

6 Click the folder to which you want to add the bookmark or click **Bookmarks Bar** if you want it to appear in the Safari Bookmark menu bar.

7 Click **Add**.

● If you clicked **Bookmarks Bar** in step 6, the new bookmark appears first in the list on the Safari Bookmarks menu bar.

Note: Clicking the new bookmark automatically loads the associated Web page.

ORGANIZE YOUR BOOKMARKS

① Click **Bookmarks**.

② Click **Show All Bookmarks**.

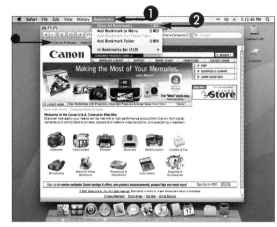

The Bookmarks window appears.

③ Click the item in the sidebar under Bookmarks that you want to organize.

④ Click and drag an item to a different location or to a different folder.

● For the Bookmarks bar, you can click and drag bookmarks to make them appear at a different spot on the bar.

● You can also add new folders by clicking under Collections and Bookmarks.

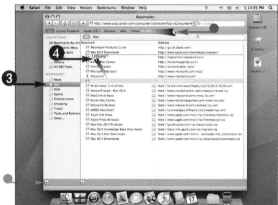

TIPS

Are there shortcuts for adding and editing bookmarks?

Yes. Pressing ⌘+D in Safari selects the current page and opens the Add Bookmarks dialog box. You can quickly access all the bookmarks by clicking the **Show All Bookmarks** button (📖) at the left side of the Bookmarks bar.

How do I remove a bookmark?

You can move a bookmark from the Bookmarks bar to another folder by clicking and dragging it in the Bookmarks window to another folder. You can delete a bookmark by highlighting it and pressing Delete or by clicking and dragging it to the desktop Trash.

Using Tabbed Browsing

Usually, opening a new Web page replaces the previous one. This makes comparing pages cumbersome. You could open a new page in a separate window, but this quickly clutters the screen with too many windows. Safari offers a better way to keep Web pages organized with tabbed browsing. When you use this feature, each Web page loads into tabs in the same window, making Web surfing much faster.

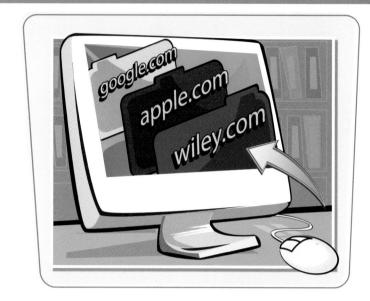

Using Tabbed Browsing

SET UP TAB PREFERENCES

① In Safari, click **Safari**.

② Click **Preferences**.

The Safari Preferences window opens.

③ Click **Tabs**.

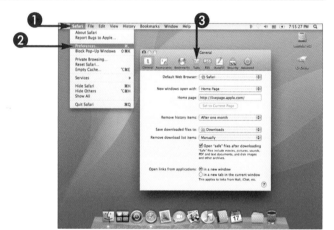

④ Click **⌘-click opens a link in a new tab** (☐ changes to ☑) if it is not already selected.

⑤ Click **Select tabs and windows as they are created** (☐ changes to ☑).

⑥ Click ⊙.

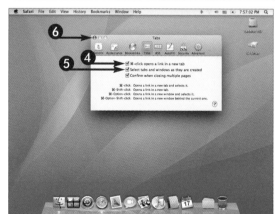

USE TABS TO BROWSE

1 In a Safari window, press 🖰 and click a link.

● The linked page opens in a new tab.

2 Press 🖰+🅣.

● An untitled Safari tab opens with a blank URL field.

3 Type a new Web address.

4 Press Return.

Safari loads the new page as a tab in the window.

TIPS

I changed the Tab Preferences, and now the usual shortcuts do not seem to work. Why?

Changing the tab options in Safari's Preferences automatically changes the default shortcuts, depending on the options that you selected. You can view the current shortcuts in the Tabs pane of the Preferences.

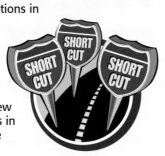

How do I open a page in a new separate window?

To open a new separate Safari window, press 🖰+🅝. The current open Web page will then be shown in both windows; to go to a new page, press 🖰+🅛 to highlight the Address bar, type the page name and suffix that you want, and press Return.

View
RSS Feeds

RSS is a technology enabling end users to subscribe to specific Web sites and stay current with new information as it is updated. RSS feed capabilities are built in to Mac OS X Leopard's Safari. Safari enables you to read RSS feeds and also to bookmark them, so you can quickly get the latest information about a particular topic.

View RSS Feeds

LOAD AN RSS FEED

① In Safari, click **News** in the Bookmarks bar.

② Click **View All RSS Articles**.

A page opens with headlines from all the listed news agencies.

③ Click a headline in the RSS feed.

Safari opens the related Web page.

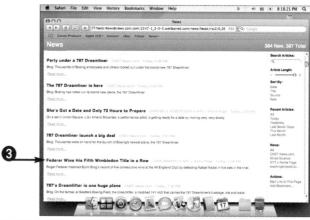

USE AN RSS BOOKMARK

1 Click .

The Bookmarks window appears.

2 In the sidebar, click **All RSS Feeds**.

An alphabetized list of RSS feeds appears.

3 Double-click an RSS feed listing.

Safari opens the RSS page.

Note: *You can bookmark any RSS feed by following the steps in "Organize Web Sites with Bookmarks," earlier in this chapter.*

TIPS

How can I tell if a Web page offers an RSS feed?

When you open a Web page with an associated RSS feed, the URL field includes the blue RSS button (RSS). Click the button, and the RSS page loads.

Can I change the amount of information displayed on an RSS feed and include photos?

You can move the Article Length slider in the sidebar of the RSS feed page to increase or decrease the amount of content displayed. You can also use the sidebar tools to sort the information. RSS feeds do not include photos or graphics.

You may find a Web page that you want to save as a reference or just to read at a later date. Saving Web pages is particularly useful before traveling when you may be without an Internet connection and need the information from a particular Web site. You can save Web pages as a Web archive or as a page source.

Save a Web Page

1 In Safari, open a Web page to save.

2 Click **File**.

3 Click **Save As**.

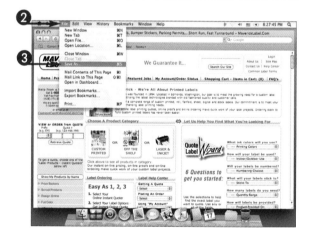

A dialog box appears.

4 Type a name for the page.

5 Click the Where ▴▾.

A list of general locations and recently used locations on your hard drive appears.

6 Click a location in which to save the Web page.

● You can also click here to expand the dialog box and view more saving options.

7 Click the Format ⬍ and select **Web Archive**.

8 Click **Save**.

The Web page is saved in the specified location with an Archive icon ().

TIP

What is the difference between choosing Web Archive and Page Source from the Format ⬍?

Saving as a Web archive maintains all the graphics as well as the text. Links in a Web archive page remain active as long as the linked Web pages are still available and there is an Internet connection. Saving a page in the Page Source format saves only the text of the page and the HTML source code. Saving as a page source is used most often to copy HTML code from one Web page to create and design a new Web page.

Customize Your Email Accounts

The first time that you started up Mac OS X Leopard, you probably created an email account. You can add other email accounts in the Preferences of the Mail application and customize the way that each mailbox handles incoming and outgoing email. Leopard also enables you to customize Mail's toolbar to keep you organized.

Customize Your Email Accounts

ADD AN EMAIL ACCOUNT

① Click the Mail button ( ) in the Dock.

The Mail application launches.

② Click **File**.

③ Click **Add Account**.

The New Account dialog box appears.

④ Type the name, email address, and password in the fields.

⑤ Click **Create**.

*Note: For an account other than a .Mac account, Incoming and Outgoing Mail Server dialog boxes open. Enter the requested data and click **Continue**.*

Mail searches the servers and creates the account.

Note: Your ISP provides the account type and incoming and outgoing mail server information.

⑥ Click **Done** in the final dialog box.

**CUSTOMIZE HOW MAIL HANDLES
YOUR EMAIL**

① In Mail, click **Mail**.

② Click **Preferences**.

The Mail Preferences window appears.

③ Click **Accounts**.

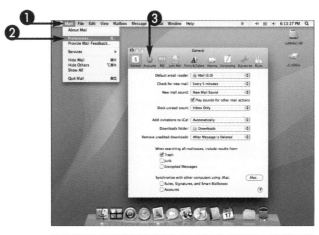

The Mail Accounts Preferences appear.

④ Click an email account.

⑤ Click **Mailbox Behaviors**.

⑥ Click check boxes to set your particular preferences (☐ changes to ☑).

⑦ Click ⬍s to change any of the other options.

⑧ Click ⦿.

⑨ Click **Save** in the confirmation box that appears.

Your email will now be managed according to the options that you chose.

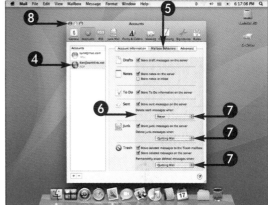

 TIP

How do I customize my Mail toolbar?

In the Mail menu bar, click **View → Customize Toolbar**. A selection of icons appears in a dialog box. Click and drag any icon you want to see in the Mail toolbar. You can place the added tools anywhere on the toolbar. To remove any tool, including the default tools, click and drag the tool icon away from the toolbar. It disappears in a puff of smoke. You can always click and drag the original default set back into the toolbar. Click **Done** when your toolbar includes all the tools you want.

Create and Send
an Email Message

Our world today revolves around email. Mac OS X Leopard's easy-to-use Mail application integrates with the Address Book and simplifies the composition and sending of emails.

Create and Send an Email Message

SEND EMAIL TO ONE RECIPIENT

1 In the Mail application, click **File**.

2 Click **New Message**.

● Alternatively, you can click **New Message** in the Mail toolbar.

Mail opens a new message window.

3 Click in the To: field and type an address.

Note: Mail automatically starts filling in the address as you type if it is in the Address Book.

4 Click in the Subject: field and type the subject heading.

5 Click in the blank message area and type the message.

6 Click the **Send** button (▨).

Mail sends the email message.

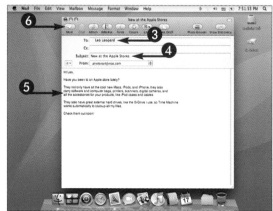

SEND EMAIL TO MULTIPLE RECIPIENTS AT ONE TIME

1 Perform the preceding steps **1** to **3**.

2 Type a comma.

Note: If Mail automatically fills in the address correctly, press Enter *and type a second address without first entering a comma.*

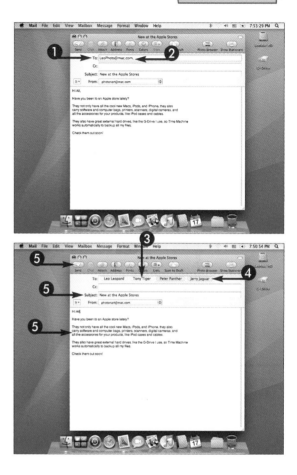

3 Type a second email address.

4 Repeat step **3** until all the addresses are in the To: field, separated by commas.

5 Perform the preceding steps **4** to **6**.

Mail sends the email message to all the recipients.

 TIPS

Is there another way to add addresses quickly?

You can click the **Address** button (⬛) in the Mail toolbar. A small Address Book appears; click a name to add to the Address field. Repeat this until you have entered all the intended recipients of the email.

Can I send carbon copies to other addresses?

Yes. To do so, simply add the addresses in the Cc: field. You can also send blind carbon copies to others whose addresses will not be seen by the main recipient. To add a Bcc: field, click the Customize Header button (⬛) in the lower-left corner of the address area and select **Bcc Address Field**.

Work with Email Attachments

Leopard's Mail application makes it easy to attach a photo or other document to any email. When you receive an email with attachments, Mail enables you to save the attachment to your hard drive and even view multiple attachments as a slideshow, which is perfect for viewing attached photos.

Work with Email Attachments

ATTACH A FILE TO AN EMAIL

① Create a new email as shown in steps **1** to **5** of the previous task; however, do not click **Send**.

② Click **Attach** (🖼).

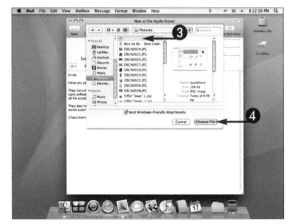

A navigation window appears.

③ Navigate to and click the file to attach.

④ Click **Choose File**.

The attached file appears in the message.

Note: *The attachment appears at the last location of the cursor in the email.*

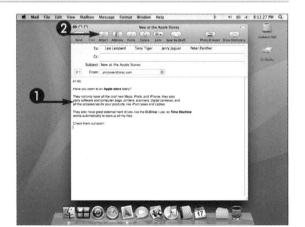

SAVE AN ATTACHMENT RECEIVED WITH AN EMAIL

1 In Mail, click **Inbox**.

Mail displays a list of the email messages in the Inbox.

● Alternatively, you can click **File** and click **New Viewer Window**.

2 Click the message with the attachment.

Mail displays the message in the bottom pane.

Note: You may need to click and drag the bottom separator line up toward the top to see the message.

3 Click **Save**.

4 Click **Save All**.

5 Navigate to and select the location to save the attachments and click **Save**.

Optionally, click only one of the attachments, or if you have iPhoto installed, click **Add to iPhoto** to add any images to your iPhoto library automatically.

Mail saves the attached file to the specified location.

TIPS

How do I prevent Mail from automatically downloading my email?

You can set the Mail application to check for mail manually or at specific intervals of time. Click **Mail →** **Preferences**. Click **General** to view the overall settings. Click the Check for New Mail and click **Manually**. Click the Close button ( ) to complete the setting.

What happens if I click the Slideshow button next to the attachment?

Clicking the **Slideshow** button makes all the attached files automatically appear as a continuous running slideshow against a black screen. Press Spacebar to bring up the slideshow controls so that you can advance the attachments manually, fill the screen with an image, or stop the show. Clicking **Slideshow** does not save the file.

Delete an Email Message

Deleting old email messages leaves your Inbox less cluttered, making it easier to find important messages and saving hard drive space. You can move email messages from your Inbox to the Trash in various ways. However, to remove them completely from your hard drive, you must empty the Mail application's Trash.

Delete an Email Message

MOVE AN EMAIL TO THE TRASH WITH THE KEYBOARD

1. In Mail, click a message to select it.
2. Press Delete or click Delete ( ).

   Mail moves the message to the Trash folder.

DRAG AN EMAIL TO THE TRASH

1. In Mail, click a message to select it.
2. Drag the email to the Mail Trash folder.

   Mail moves the message to the Trash folder.

EMPTY THE TRASH

❶ Click **Mailbox**.

❷ Click **Erase Deleted Messages**.

❸ Click **In All Accounts**.

Mail deletes all the emails in the Trash folder and from your hard drive.

DELETE ONE EMAIL FROM THE TRASH

❶ Click **Trash**.

❷ Click an email in the Trash.

❸ Press Delete or click 🚫.

Mail deletes the one email from the Trash folder and from your hard drive.

Note: Press ⌘ +click to select more than one email or press ⌘ + A to select all the emails in step **2** before pressing Delete to remove multiple emails from your hard drive.

I accidentally moved an important email to the Trash. How do I recover it?

You can retrieve an email from the Trash by clicking **Trash** and then clicking and dragging the email to another folder in the window or back to the Inbox.

Does deleting the email and emptying the Trash completely erase the email?

Emails may be saved on your Internet service provider's server even after you delete them from your computer. To permanently delete the messages on the server when you empty the Mail Trash, click **Mail → Preferences**. In the Accounts Preferences, click **Mailbox Behaviors**. Uncheck the box in the Trash section, next to **Store deleted messages on the server** (☑ changes to ☐).

Personalize Your Emails with Stationery

Mac OS X Leopard's Mail application enables you to send colorful and personalized emails without using any separate specialized computer graphics applications. Mail makes it easy with stationery templates for a variety of different looks. You can also add your own photos to any of the included stationery templates for a customized look.

Personalize Your Emails with Stationery

USE A STATIONERY TEMPLATE

1 In Mail, click **File**.

2 Click **New Message**.

A new blank message window appears.

3 Type the recipients' email addresses and the subject heading in the corresponding fields.

4 Click **Show Stationery** ().

A list of types of stationery with a display of each one appears.

5 Click a category, such as **Birthday**.

6 Click the stationery that you want.

Note: *Depending on the size of the window, you may have to scroll the stationery display bar to the right.*

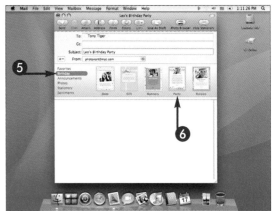

The message area fills with the template.

7 Double-click the supplied placeholder header.

8 Type the text that you want to appear.

9 Click and drag across the main placeholder text to highlight it.

10 Type your own text.

ADD YOUR OWN PHOTO

11 Click in the Dock.

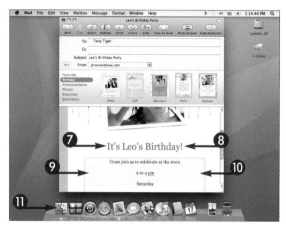

The Finder window appears.

12 Navigate to the folder with your photos.

13 Click and drag the photo that you want over the placeholder.

14 Click  to send the mail.

Note: You can also click **Photo Browser** (⬚) to open your iPhoto library. Click and drag an image onto the placeholder in the email stationery.

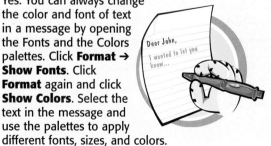

TIPS

Can people who do not have Leopard or who are using PCs see the personalized email stationery?

Yes. Everyone who receives your email sees your customized and colorful message, including the photos, as long as the mail client they are using supports HTML and not just text.

Can I change the color of the text and font style in the stationery template?

Yes. You can always change the color and font of text in a message by opening the Fonts and the Colors palettes. Click **Format →** **Show Fonts**. Click **Format** again and click **Show Colors**. Select the text in the message and use the palettes to apply different fonts, sizes, and colors.

Using Mail Notes

Mac OS X Leopard adds a new Notes feature to the Mail application. Notes are perfect for writing down brainstorming ideas or even taking notes in a class. You can send a note to yourself to always have it accessible with your email. You can add photos to notes, and if you type a Web page address, Notes turns it into a working link when you send the note to yourself or someone else.

Using Mail Notes

① In Mail, click **File**.

② Click **New Note**.

A yellow notepad appears.

③ Type any text that you want to remember.

● You can include an Internet address as well.

● You can add a photo to your note by opening a Finder window, navigating to your photo, and clicking and dragging the photo into the note.

④ Click **Send** (Send).

The note appears in the message pane of an email window.

⑤ Type your email address in the To: field.

⑥ Click Send.

If you have an Internet connection, the note, along with any included photos or active Web page links, appears as a new email in your Inbox.

Can I just save the note without sending it?
Yes. Click **File →Save** or press ⌘+S. Click 🔘 to close the note window. The note is saved in the Notes section of your Mail window.

What is the To Do button for?
You can select some text in a note and click **To Do** (To Do) to mark it as a To Do item. Click the red arrow that appears and select the due date, priority, and calendar in the dialog box. The To Do item is then linked to your iCal calendar.

Reduce Spam in Your Inbox

Everyone with an email address receives spam or unwanted messages along with their important emails. Leopard's Mail application helps reduce the amount of spam in your Inbox by using a junk mail filter. You set the parameters of what constitutes junk mail using the Mail Preferences, and Mail marks junk mail in a selected color, making it easy to spot.

Reduce Spam in Your Inbox

SET THE JUNK MAIL PARAMETERS

1 Click **Mail**.

2 Click **Preferences**.

The Mail Preferences window appears.

3 Click **Junk Mail** (🖼️).

The Junk Mail Preferences pane opens.

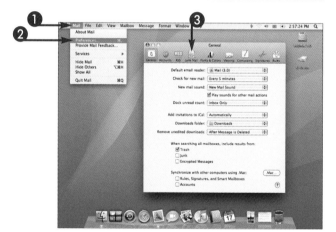

4 Click **Enable junk mail filtering** (☐ changes to ☑).

5 Click **Mark as junk mail, but leave it in my Inbox** (◯ changes to ⦿).

Note: *Check the messages in your mailbox and mark or unmark them as Junk to update the internal junk mail database and train the Mail application.*

● Optionally, click **Perform custom actions** and click **Advanced** to set specific junk filtering preferences.

6 Click 🖼️.

Now suspected spam will be marked as junk mail in your Inbox.

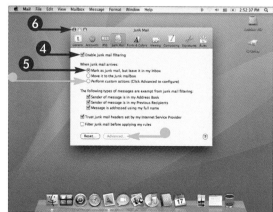

DESIGNATE MAIL AS JUNK MAIL

1 In Mail, click your Inbox.

Mail displays the messages in the Inbox.

2 Click an email message that you consider to be spam.

3 Click **Junk** ( ).

Mail marks the message as junk.

Note: Marking messages as Junk also helps train Mail to recognize junk mail.

REMOVE THE JUNK MARKER FROM AN EMAIL

1 Click an email message marked as junk that is not spam.

2 Click **Not Junk** ( ).

Mail removes the marker and changes the color.

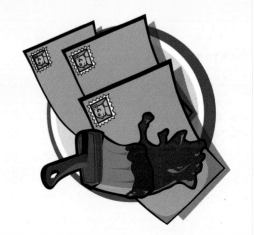

TIP

How do I change the brown junk mail color?
You can change the color that Mail applies to junk mail in your Inbox using the Mail Preferences. Click **Mail →
Preferences**. Click ▦ in the Preferences window. Click **Perform custom actions** and click the **Advanced** button in the Junk Mail pane. Click the **Other** (default brown) color square at the bottom of the next dialog box. Click a different color in the color wheel that appears. Click **OK**. Click ◉ to close the Preferences window.

CHAPTER 7

Connecting Peripherals to Your Mac

Whether your Mac is an all-in-one such as a laptop or an iMac, or a desktop tower with a separate monitor, peripheral devices include any added hardware that expands the functionality of the computer. Mac OS X Leopard makes it easy to attach and use peripherals from printers to scanners, cameras, added drives, microphones, and even different mice.

Introducing Input and Output Devices

Among the many advantages the Macintosh computer has over other types of computers is its capability to connect most peripheral devices and use them with few or no complicated steps. Mac OS X Leopard is the most advanced operating system to date and even comes with built-in applications to help you make the most of certain external devices.

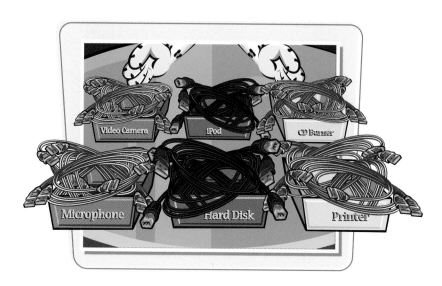

Many Types of Ports

Most peripheral devices connect with the Mac computer through its various ports, which can include USB, FireWire, Ethernet, modem, display, and audio ports. However, not all Macs come with all the different types of ports. Most Macs also include wireless technology such as Airport and Bluetooth built in, which enables them to connect to certain peripherals wirelessly without an external port.

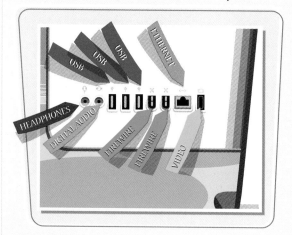

Matching Computer Cables

Each different type of computer port requires a matching type of cable with the appropriate male or female terminations to go from the peripheral device into the computer. Cables come in various lengths, and extenders exist for some types of cables to make them longer.

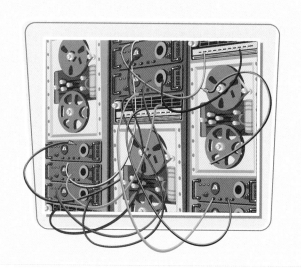

Input versus Output Devices

Keyboards, mice, and scanners are considered input devices because they send information into the computer. Printers and monitors are output devices, whereas modems, Bluetooth devices, and Ethernet devices communicate as both input and output devices.

Understanding Software Drivers

Some peripherals can function the minute that you plug them into the Mac. Others require you to install an application called a *software driver,* provided by the device manufacturer. Software drivers enable the Mac operating system to recognize and interact transparently with the device.

External Storage Devices

External storage devices include CD or DVD burners, external hard drives, USB flash drives, and media such as memory cards for digital cameras. External storage is important for storing digital images, and a high-capacity external hard drive makes an excellent backup system for use with Leopard's Time Machine.

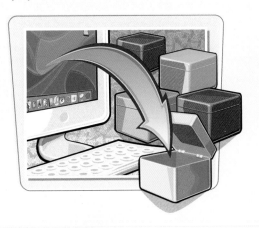

The iPod: A Special Case

The Apple iPod is an input and output device for transferring and listening to music. Mac OS X Leopard includes iTunes software to automatically interact with an iPod. iPods can also serve as external data-storage devices.

Install Drivers for Accessory Devices

Many external devices automatically work with Mac OS X Leopard through the built-in interface. If a peripheral device requires a specific software driver, the manufacturer will include a CD with the software for you to install. You can also download most drivers from the manufacturer's Web site to install them.

① Using the supplied cable, connect the peripheral device to the computer.

② Insert the peripheral device's included CD into your CD or DVD drive.

The CD appears on the desktop.

③ Double-click the CD icon to open it.

Note: *If you downloaded the software driver, navigate to the saved location and double-click its icon.*

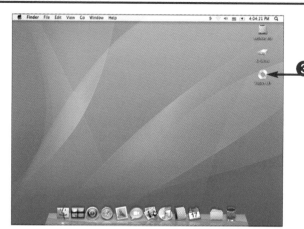

The contents of the CD appear in a Finder window.

④ Double-click the **Install** icon and follow the online steps.

Note: *Some peripheral devices include added application software on the included CD. You can elect to install the added software later.*

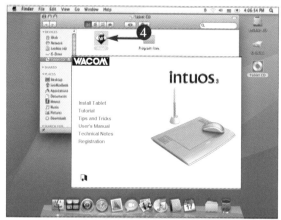

For most drivers, a licensing agreement appears.

5 Click **Agree**.

Note: Most software installations require you to agree to the licensing agreement before installing.

6 If a window appears asking you to select the destination drive, click the drive.

7 Click **Continue**.

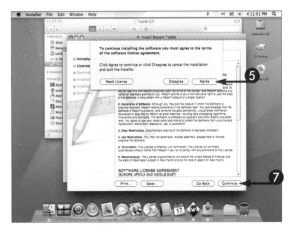

A login window appears, requesting an administrator password.

8 Type your password.

9 Click **OK**.

The installer application installs the software driver in the appropriate location.

10 Click **Finish** or **Close** in the final installation window.

11 Click **Restart** if a Restart dialog box appears.

Note: Only some software driver installations require you to restart the computer before you can use the peripheral device.

TIPS

Why does my external device no longer work since I installed Mac OS X Leopard?

The software driver must interface with both the device and the current operating system. New operating systems such as Mac OS X Leopard generally require new software drivers. Check the device manufacturer's Web site and download the latest or appropriate driver and install it.

Should I install the software driver that came on the CD in the box or the one on the manufacturer's Web site?

Because both the operating system and the peripheral device manufacturers regularly update their software, it is generally best to download the latest software drivers from the manufacturer's Web site and install it. Even if you do not change operating systems, check the device manufacturer's Web site regularly for the latest driver downloads.

A Mac usually comes with at least two USB ports, one FireWire port, and one Ethernet port. The keyboard for desktop Macs generally includes two USB ports, one of which is intended for the mouse. If you have more peripheral devices that require the same type of port, you can add a USB or FireWire hub or an Ethernet switch or router.

USB Hubs

A USB hub is a device that connects to a USB port on a computer and has a number of open USB ports for connecting other USB devices. A bus-powered hub draws its power from the computer and does not need a separate power connection; however, many USB devices require more power than such a hub supplies.

Powered USB Hubs

A powered USB hub has its own power adapter. Like the bus-powered hub, it connects to the computer's USB port and enables you to connect multiple USB devices and even another USB hub to make more ports available.

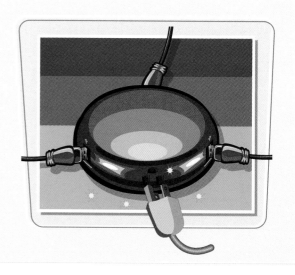

FireWire Hubs

You can usually connect multiple FireWire devices to one Macintosh using a FireWire hub. FireWire devices require a lot of power, so the hub and the devices should have separate power adapters.

Daisy-Chained FireWire Devices

You can connect multiple FireWire devices in a chain with only one device connected to the computer. Only one device can use the computer's power. The others in the chain should be powered by their own power adapters.

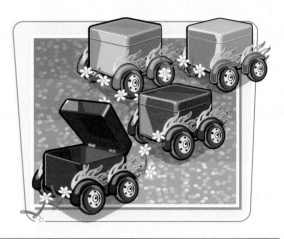

Ethernet Switches and Hubs

Ethernet hubs and switches connect multiple computers and other devices, such as printers, forming a local area network (LAN) for exchanging files. With hubs, data collisions can occur when computers on the network send data at the same time. Switches keep data flowing separately through high-speed electronics.

Ethernet Routers

Routers connect the computer to a DSL or cable modem for broadband Internet service using a wide area network (WAN) port. Many routers are combined with switches or hubs and include several ports to connect multiple computers and other Ethernet devices.

Using a pen tablet rather than a mouse enables you to move the cursor and select items with added control. Using a pen is also more ergonomic and precise than a computer mouse. You can customize pen tablets such as the Graphire or Intuos from Wacom using the Tablet settings in System Preferences.

Control Your Mac with a Pen Instead of a Mouse

① Install the tablet driver following the steps in the section "Install Drivers for Accessory Devices," earlier in this chapter.

② Click the Apple icon (🍎) and click System Preferences.

The System Preferences window appears.

③ Click **Pen Tablet**.

● Click **Wacom Tablet** for a Wacom Intuos model (but **Pen Tablet** for a Wacom Graphire model). Other pen tablets may have a different name for the Tablet Preferences.

The Tablet Preferences appear.

④ Click **Pen**.

The Pen settings appear.

⑤ Click and drag the Tip Feel 🖊 to the left for a softer pen touch or to the right for a firmer pen touch.

⑥ Click the top 🔽 and select **Keystroke**.

Note: You can select any combinations and change any of the individual Tablet Preferences.

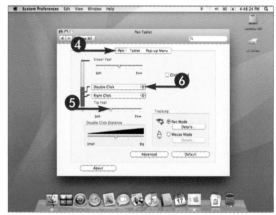

A dialog box appears.

7 Press ⌘+A.

● The appropriate symbol and letter appear in the Keys field.

8 Click **OK**.

Now pressing the top button on the pen while hovering over the tablet has the same effect as pressing the keyboard keys ⌘+A.

Note: *Other models including the Wacom Intuos have slightly different Preferences options.*

9 Click **Tablet**.

The Tablet button settings appear.

10 Click the left ⬍ and choose what you want to happen when you press the left tablet button.

11 Repeat step **10** for the right ⬍.

● You can click **Default** on any Tablet Preferences pane to reset the tablet to the original settings.

12 Click ⬤ to close the System Preferences window.

Your tablet is customized with your settings and ready to use.

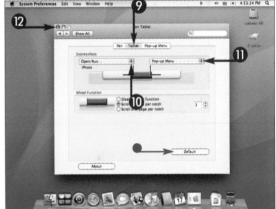

TIPS

What is the difference between a Graphire and an Intuos Wacom tablet?
The Graphire is slightly less pressure sensitive and has fewer customizable settings than the Intuos tablet. It is perfect for having fun with your photos. The Intuos is better for serious photographers, designers, and artists and comes in more tablet sizes.

Is there a quick way to learn to use the pen tablet?
Hold the pen as you would any writing instrument. Rest your hand in the center of the tablet. To move the cursor on the screen, hover or move the pen tip just above the tablet without touching it. To click, lightly tap the pen on the tablet surface. Always focus on the cursor on your screen and avoid looking at your hand.

Add a Printer

Mac OS X Leopard includes many printer drivers. If your printer's driver is already in the system, you can simply plug the printer into the appropriate port. Other printers may require you to install a specific driver. Either way, you can add and set up a printer with just a few steps.

Add a Printer

① Connect the printer to the computer with the appropriate cable.

② Turn on the printer.

③ Click .

④ Click **System Preferences**.

The System Preferences window opens.

⑤ Click **Print & Fax**.

The Print & Fax Preferences pane opens.

6 Click ⊞.

A printer browser appears.

7 Click the name of your printer.

The computer opens the connection with the printer.

8 Click **Add**.

The computer adds the printer to the Print & Fax Preferences list.

9 Click 🔘 to close System Preferences and save your settings.

 TIPS

My printer uses a USB connection. Are there other kinds?

You can have a printer connected directly to your computer using a USB or FireWire cable. You can also use a printer connected through networks such as Bonjour, Appletalk, Bluetooth, and IP (Internet protocol), as well as printers shared over a network, including printers attached to a Windows PC computer. Mac OS X Leopard can automatically find and help you set up most types of printers.

What is on the Sharing tab in the Printers & Fax Preferences pane?

When your printer is connected directly to one computer, you can print with it from another computer as long as the computers are connected to each other or through a network. In the Print & Fax Preferences, click the printer that you want to share to select it. Click **Share this printer** (☐ changes to ☑).

Print Documents

Using the Page Setup and Print functions in Mac OS X Leopard, you can quickly adjust a variety of settings to print documents exactly the way that you want. You can adjust the page size of the print job, the orientation of the page, and, depending on the application, the number of copies to be printed.

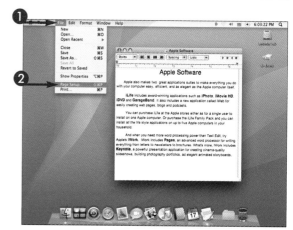

Print Documents

CHANGE THE PAGE SETUP

① With the document open that you want to print, click **File**.

② Click **Page Setup**.

The Page Setup dialog box appears.

③ Click the Format For ⬍ and select your printer's name.

④ Click the Paper Size ⬍ and select the paper size.

⑤ Click portrait (⬛) or landscape (⬛) orientation.

⑥ Click **OK**.

The Page Setup dialog box closes.

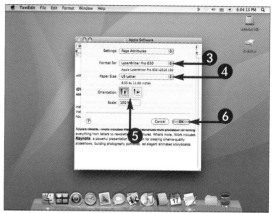

PRINT THE DOCUMENT

① Click **File**.

② Click **Print**.

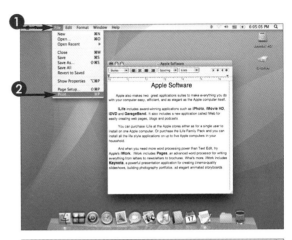

The Print dialog box appears.

③ Click ▾.

The Print dialog box expands.

④ Double-click here and type the number of copies to print if more than one copy is needed.

● If necessary, you can click **From** (○ changes to ◉) and type the specific page range to print.

⑤ Click **Print**.

The document is printed.

 TIPS

What does the ⬍ by the application name under the Orientation buttons do?

You can select any special features of your printer such as double-sided or duplex printing, printing a cover page, and scheduling the printing by clicking that ⬍ and selecting the various options.

Can I print to a nonstandard paper size?

You can use a custom size if your printer offers this feature. Click the Paper Size ⬍ in the Page Setup dialog box and select **Manage Custom Sizes**. Click ⊞ to add a paper size. Type a name, width, and height for the custom size. Specify the margins in the fields. Click **OK**. The new paper size is now listed in the Page Setup dialog box.

Mount a Laptop As a Disk Drive and Copy Its Files

You can connect two Macs together to transfer files using a FireWire cable. In *Target disk mode,* as this is called, the target computer appears as an external hard disk on the host computer. Target disk mode is often used for quickly transferring large files between a laptop and another computer.

Mount a Laptop As a Disk Drive and Copy Its Files

CONNECT A LAPTOP TARGET DISK

1. Shut down the laptop target computer.

2. Power on the host computer.

3. Connect the two computers with a FireWire cable.

4. Press and hold **T** on the laptop target computer as you press its power button.

   The target laptop turns on.

5. Release **T** when you see the FireWire icon floating on the laptop screen.

   The target disk's hard drive appears on the desktop of the host computer.

6. Click **Ignore** in the dialog box that appears.

Note: *The Enable Time Machine dialog box appears anytime a sufficiently large drive is mounted and the Time Machine is not already enabled.*

COPY FILES FROM THE TARGET DISK

1. Double-click the target disk.

A Finder window appears with the target disk's contents.

② Navigate to the files or folders to copy.

③ Click and drag the files from the target disk to the host computer's Home folder.

Note: *You can also click and drag files from the host computer to the target disk.*

EJECT AND DISCONNECT A TARGET DISK

① Click and drag the target disk's icon to the Trash.

The target disk is ejected.

② Turn off the power to the target disk.

③ Disconnect the FireWire cable.

TIPS

Why would I use Target disk mode rather than an Ethernet connection?

Transferring large files is faster using a FireWire cable in Target disk mode. To connect two Macintosh computers to share files by Ethernet, you need to connect an Ethernet cable from the Ethernet port on one computer to the other or use an Ethernet router, switch, or hub. You must turn on Personal File Sharing on both computers.

Other than file transfer, does Target disk mode have other uses?

Yes. You can also use Target disk mode to troubleshoot the target disk computer's operating system. In Target disk mode, you have complete access to the system and files on the target disk, as long as FileVault is not enabled. See Chapter 10 for an explanation of FileVault.

Start Your Mac from a Different Drive or a CD/DVD

Your computer's built-in hard drive is generally the main startup drive. You can start up from a separate internal or external drive including FireWire drives and CD or DVD drives, when these have a system installed. Starting up from a separate drive is useful for installing new systems and certain software and for troubleshooting or repairing the internal startup drive.

Start Your Mac from a Different Drive or a CD/DVD

START UP FROM A DIFFERENT HARD DRIVE

1 Connect a separate FireWire hard drive with Mac OS X Leopard installed.

Note: Depending on your Mac, you may be able to start up from an earlier version of Mac OS X.

Note: You can use a USB drive as a startup drive, but only on Intel-based Macs. You can also use a second built-in hard drive if it has an operating system installed.

2 Click ![apple].

3 Click **Restart**.

4 Press and hold Option as soon as the screen goes dark.

A plain screen appears, showing all the available startup systems.

Note: It can take a while for all the available drives to appear.

5 Click the startup drive that you want.

6 Click the arrow.

Note: You can also press Return.

The Mac boots from the selected drive.

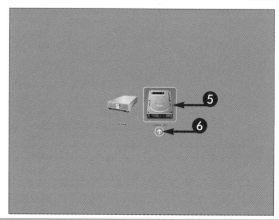

START UP FROM A CD/DVD DRIVE

1 Insert a CD or DVD with Mac OS X Leopard installed into your CD/DVD drive.

Note: Depending on your Macintosh model, you may be able to start up from a CD or DVD with an earlier version of Mac OS X, such as 10.4 Tiger.

2 Click .

3 Click System Preferences.

The System Preferences window appears.

4 Click **Startup Disk**.

5 Click the system startup disc.

6 Click **Restart**.

The Mac boots from the operating system on the CD or DVD.

TIP

Are there other ways to boot up from separate CDs or DVDs?

You can also insert a CD or DVD with a startup system on it. Click → **Restart**. As soon as the screen goes dark, press and hold and keep holding it until the system starts up. This method can be easier than changing the startup disk in System Preferences because after you change the startup disk in System Preferences, you must repeat the steps before you restart or before you shut down the computer.

Copy Music to an iPod

With Mac OS X Leopard and an iPod, you can easily take all your favorite music with you anywhere. Leopard includes the iTunes application, making it easy to import and organize your music. When you plug in an iPod, you can automatically copy only selected music files or sync all your music from your computer with your iPod.

Copy Music to an iPod

COPY ALL MUSIC TO THE IPOD

1 Click 🎵.

2 Plug the iPod into a USB or FireWire port on the Macintosh.

3 If a warning appears, click **Erase and Sync**.

The iPod's contents are erased and replaced with the computer's iTunes library.

COPY SPECIFIC MUSIC FILES

4 Click the iPod icon.

5 On the Music tab, click **Selected playlists**.

6 Click the playlists you want.

7 Click **Sync**.

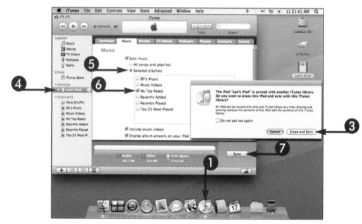

DISCONNECT THE IPOD CORRECTLY

1 If the iPod screen shows the main menu or a battery icon, disconnect the iPod cable.

OR

1 If the iPod screen shows the Do Not Disconnect screen, click **iPod** in the iTunes Source list.

2 Click the **Eject iPod** button (⏏).

The iPod displays the OK to Disconnect screen.

3 Disconnect the iPod cable.

In addition to storing and playing music, your iPod can also store files. Using your iPod as an external storage disk enables you to transfer files between two computers, but you can still use it as a music player. The maximum size of files that you can store depends on the iPod model and the number of other files you have on it.

Store Files on an iPod

1 In iTunes, click **iPod** in the Source pane.

The Summary window appears.

2 Click **Enable disk use** (☐ changes to ☑).

3 Click **Apply**.

4 Press ⌘+Q to quit iTunes.

The iPod icon appears on the Desktop.

5 Click 🎵 in the Dock.

6 Navigate to the files to transfer.

7 Double-click the **iPod** icon to open the iPod window.

8 Click and drag files from your computer to the iPod window.

9 Click and drag the **iPod** icon to the Trash.

The iPod is ejected and can be disconnected safely.

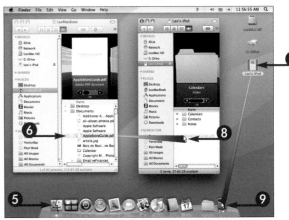

Using an External Microphone with iChat

The new iChat AV in Mac OS X Leopard enables you to have a conversation over the Internet without typing. You can have an audio iChat with up to ten people or a video iChat with up to four people. You can attach an external microphone even if your Mac has a built-in one to enhance your Internet conversation.

Using an External Microphone with iChat

① Connect a microphone to the USB, FireWire, or built-in audio port on your Macintosh computer.

Note: *Follow the same steps below if you have a built-in microphone.*

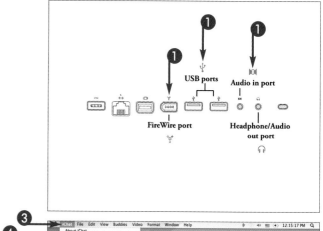

② Click the iChat icon (🔵) in the Dock.

The iChat application launches, and the Buddy List appears.

Note: *If this is the first time that you are launching iChat, set up your account in the dialog boxes and click **Done**.*

③ Click **iChat**.

④ Click **Preferences**.

The iChat Preferences window opens.

5 Click **Audio/Video**.

6 Click the Microphone ⬍ and select your microphone.

7 Click 🔘.

The iChat Preferences window closes.

8 Click a buddy with a Telephone or Camera icon next to his or her name.

9 Click the Telephone icon (📞).

iChat initiates an audio connection.

How can I make my conversation more secure?

If you and your buddies each have a .Mac account, you can set up encrypted iChat conversations. Not only your audio chats but also your text messages and video chats are encrypted, or locked, preventing uninvited listeners from hearing or viewing your conversation.

What kinds of microphones can I use with iChat?

You can use almost any kind of external microphone as long as it has the proper hardware to interface with the Mac. Some newer external microphones include USB adapters. The microphones built in to external FireWire video cameras, including Apple's iSight, are also compatible with iChat. You can test an attached microphone in the Video pane of the iChat Preferences window.

Conduct a Video Chat with an External Video Camera

If you and your iChat buddies each have a FireWire camera connected to your computers, you can have a video chat. Some laptop Macs and iMacs come with a camera built-in to the bezel of the monitor. You can also connect an external MiniDV camera if it has a FireWire connection.

Conduct a Video Chat with an External Video Camera

① Connect a video camera to the FireWire port on your Macintosh.

② Turn on the video camera.

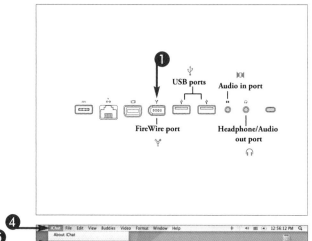

③ Click 💬 in the Dock.

The iChat application launches.

④ Click **iChat**.

⑤ Click **Preferences**.

The iChat Preferences window opens.

⑥ Click **Audio/Video**.

The Audio/Video Preferences pane opens.

⑦ Click **Automatically open iChat when external camera is turned on** (☐ changes to ☑).

An image appears in the video preview pane.

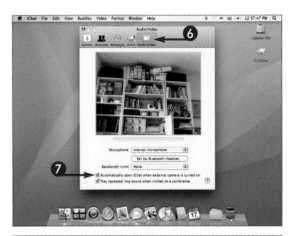

⑧ Press ⌘+1 to open your Buddy List if it is not already open.

⑨ Click a buddy in the list.

⑩ Click the buddy's Camera icon (▣).

iChat initiates a video connection.

TIP

What if my buddy does not have a camera attached?

You can conduct a text chat, an audio chat if both parties have a built-in or external microphone, or even a one-way video chat if only one of you has a camera attached or built in. The buddy with the camera must initiate the chat. Click a buddy in the Buddy List. Click **Buddies → Invite to One-Way Video Chat**. iChat sends an invitation to chat to the buddy without the camera. When the buddy accepts, he or she will see and hear you in the video preview window.

8

Listening to Music, Radio, and Podcasts

With the iTunes application that comes with Mac OS X Leopard, you can listen to music and podcasts on your Mac. Included are tools for organizing your music collection, viewing album covers, burning a CD, and printing a content-related CD cover insert. With each new version of iTunes, Apple adds even more features, so iTunes may look slightly different than what is shown here.

Mac OS X Leopard is so versatile that it offers you many options for listening to music. If you just want to listen to or identify a music file, you can preview the music from within the Finder without launching a separate music-editing application.

Preview Music from the Finder

① In the Finder or a Finder window, navigate to and click the audio file to highlight it.

② Click **File**.

③ Click **Get Info**.

Note: If the Finder window is in Column view, the preview player appears in the far-right column when a music file is highlighted.

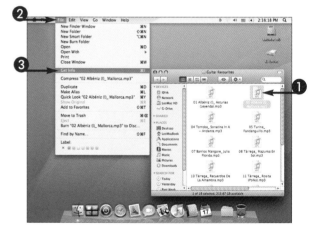

The Info window for the file appears.

④ Click the Preview ▶.

A black square with musical notes appears.

5 Move the cursor over the center of the notes.

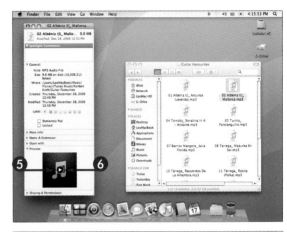

appears.

6 Click.

The audio file plays, and changes to.

7 Click to stop the playback.

TIPS

What kinds of audio files can I play in the Get Info window?

Get Info will play all the most-common audio file formats, including MP3, AIFF, WAV, and AAC. The Get Info window will not display a preview player for any file type that cannot be played.

Can I use any keyboard shortcuts when I preview music with the Get Info window?

Yes. You can open the Get Info window for any selected file by pressing ⌘+I.

Listen to Music with the QuickTime Player

The QuickTime Player is a multimedia player used for audio, video, and even still images. Although the QuickTime Player is most often used to view movies, you can also use it to play a soundtrack and many audio formats. Playing music in QuickTime enables you to control the playback sound balances as well as the volume, bass, and treble levels.

Listen to Music with the QuickTime Player

① In the Finder, press ⌘ + Ⓐ.

The Applications window appears.

② Press Ⓠ and navigate to the QuickTime application.

③ Press Option and double-click the QuickTime Player icon.

The QuickTime player opens, and the Applications window closes.

Optionally, you can click ⊙ to close the QuickTime window.

④ Click **File**.

⑤ Click **Open File**.

The Open dialog box appears.

⑥ Navigate to the location of the audio file that you want to listen to.

⑦ Click the audio file.

⑧ Click **Open**.

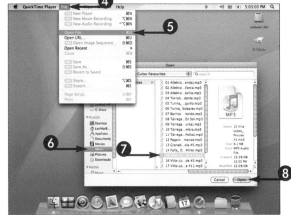

The QuickTime Player opens the audio file in its own player window.

9 Click ▶.

The audio file plays, and ▶ changes to ⏸.

10 Click ⏸.

The audio file stops playing.

Note: *You can also press* Spacebar *to start and stop the player.*

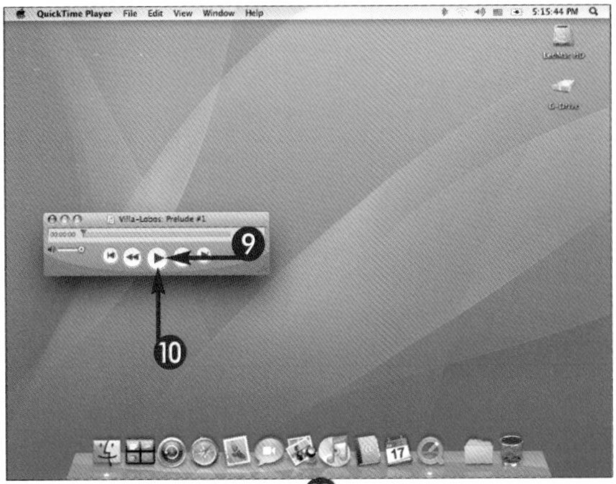

11 Click **Window**.

12 Click **Show A/V Controls**.

The A/V Controls window opens.

13 Click and drag any slider to adjust the sound.

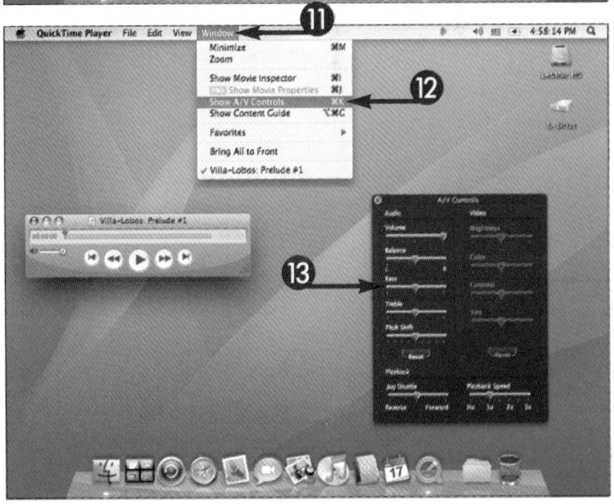

TIPS

Are there keyboard shortcuts to change the volume?

Yes. In addition to pressing Spacebar to start and stop the player, you can press ↑ to increase the volume and ↓ to decrease the volume.

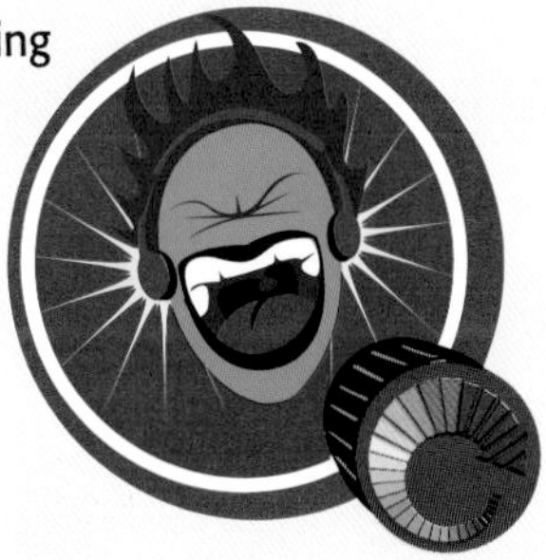

What types of audio files can the QuickTime Player play?

The QuickTime Player can play the most-common audio file formats, including AIFF/AIFC, audio CD, CAF, MOV, MP2, MP3, MPEG-4, AU, WAV, and iTunes music.

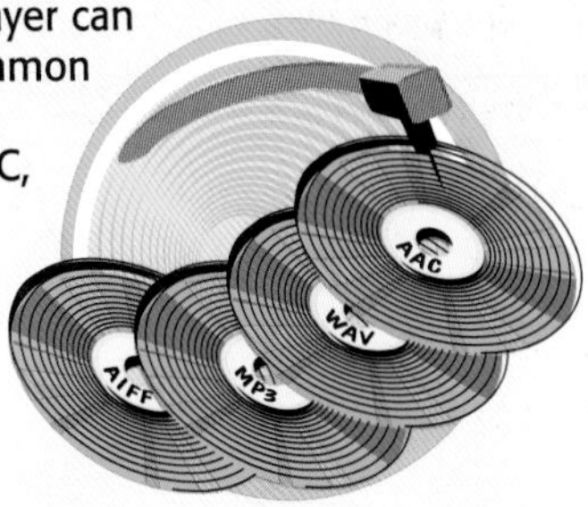

Listen to Music with iTunes

Mac OS X Leopard includes the iTunes application. iTunes acts as a personal jukebox, which you can use to listen to a song or a list of songs from your iTunes library or any other audio file on your computer. You can also insert a music CD and use iTunes to play any or all of the music on the disc.

Listen to Music with iTunes

PLAY A SONG

1 In the Dock, click the iTunes icon ().

The iTunes application launches.

2 Click **Music**.

iTunes displays all music in the iTunes library.

3 Double-click the song that you want to hear.

The song plays.

4 Click the Advance button (▶▶).

The next song in the library starts playing.

5 Click ⏸.

The audio file stops playing.

REPEAT A SONG OR A PLAYLIST

1 Double-click the song.

The song plays.

2 Click the Repeat button (⟳) once.

iTunes continues playing each song in the list and, when finished, repeats playing the list.

3 Click ⟳ again.

iTunes continuously repeats the current song.

4 Click ⟳ a third time.

iTunes deactivates the repeat playback and stops playing after the song finishes.

TIPS

How do I make iTunes play my songs in a specific order?

By clicking the column heading in the playlist, you can set iTunes to play songs in alphabetical order by song title, by artist, or by album.

How can I tell what repeat mode I am in, and is there another way to toggle the repeat modes?

If you forget how many times you pressed the Repeat button, you can look at the button. If it is blue, iTunes repeats the entire list. If the button has a small number 1 in a blue circle (⟳), iTunes repeats just the one song. You can also click **Controls** and click **Repeat Off**, **Repeat All**, or **Repeat One**.

Import Your Audio CDs

iTunes enables you to import music from your CDs as well as purchase and download songs from the Internet. You can import an entire album or select individual songs to add to your computer's music library. After the songs are imported into iTunes, you can play and organize your music any way that you want.

Import Your Audio CDs

IMPORT AN ENTIRE ALBUM

① Insert the music CD into the CD/DVD drive on your Macintosh.

● iTunes launches. The CD appears under the Devices heading, and the list of songs appears in the iTunes window.

② Click **Import CD**.

iTunes automatically imports the songs into your iTunes library.

Note: *iTunes plays the songs as it is importing them.*

● iTunes marks each song with ⊘ after it is imported.

③ When the import is finished, click the Eject button (⏏).

● Alternatively, you can click the CD icon on the desktop to select it and click this Eject button (⏏).

IMPORT SELECTED SONGS

1 Insert the music CD into your CD/DVD drive.

If iTunes is already open, a dialog box appears, asking if you would like to import the CD into your iTunes library.

2 Click **No**.

3 Click the check box in front of the song or songs that you do not want to import (☑ changes to ☐).

4 Click **Import CD**.

iTunes imports only the selected song or songs into the library.

Note: *You can cancel importing by clicking the small X next to the progress bar at the top of the iTunes window.*

TIP

Can I make the CD automatically begin playing when I put it in my CD drive?

Yes, even though the default setting in iTunes Preferences is to open a dialog box asking if you would like to import the CD into your iTunes library when a CD is inserted. You can change this default setting to automatically begin playing each time a music CD is inserted by clicking **iTunes → Preferences**. In the iTunes Preferences window, click **Advanced**. Click the **Importing** tab and click the On CD Insert ⬍. Click **Begin Playing** and click **OK**. From now on, each time that you insert a CD, iTunes starts playing the CD.

Rip Music Files in a Different File Format and Location

By default, iTunes imports or rips music files in the AAC format, a compressed format perfect for transferring to an iPod, and saves them to the internal hard drive. You can change the default location and file format for ripping your music CD collection to give you more options for using and playing your music.

Rip Music Files in a Different File Format and Location

RIP IN A DIFFERENT FILE FORMAT

1 Click [ ].

iTunes launches.

● Optionally, you can click [ ] to close the iTunes window.

2 Click **iTunes.**

3 Click **Preferences**.

The iTunes Preferences window opens.

4 Click **Advanced**.

The Advanced Preferences pane opens.

5 Click the **Importing** tab.

The Importing Preferences pane opens.

6 Click the Import Using [ ] and select the music encoder that you want, such as **Apple Lossless Encoder**.

7 Click **OK**.

RIP MUSIC FILES TO A DIFFERENT LOCATION

Note: You may want to connect an external hard drive first to use it to store ripped files.

1 In the iTunes Advanced Preferences pane, click **General**.

2 Click **Change**.

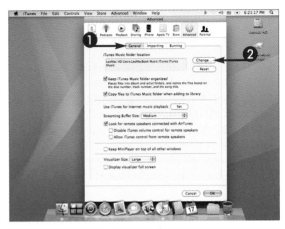

The Change Music Folder Location dialog box appears.

3 Navigate to and click a different folder or, preferably, larger external hard drive.

4 Click **Open**.

● The new location is listed in the iTunes Advanced Preferences window.

5 Click **OK** to close the iTunes Preferences window.

● You can click **Reset** to change back to the default location.

 TIP

Why should I rip my music with the Apple Lossless Encoder or a different file format than the default AAC file format and save it to an external drive?

Ripping CDs into iTunes can be time-consuming, so you should import the music in a format that can be easily converted later. The default AAC file encoder, like MP3s, compresses the files, so the files take up less room on your hard drive and on an iPod. If you plan to burn your own mixed CDs, you want the highest-quality recording. Using the Apple Lossless Encoder (ALE) creates smaller files without compromising sound quality, so the music sounds as good as your original CDs, and you can rip once and create other compressed versions later to repurpose your music collection. Saving the lossless files to a larger external hard drive gives you more options for sharing your music and saves space on your internal hard drive.

iTunes enables you to organize your music into playlists. You can create playlists of your favorite songs or playlists for special occasions. Organizing your music collection makes selecting and listening to specific songs or styles from your entire music collection quick and easy.

Build a Playlist

CREATE AND ADD SONGS TO A PLAYLIST

1 Click 🎵.

iTunes launches.

2 Click **File**.

3 Click **New Playlist**.

● Alternatively, you can click ➕.

An untitled playlist appears under the Playlist heading.

4 Type a name for the playlist.

5 Click **Music**.

6 Click and drag items from the list to the playlist.

CREATE A PLAYLIST FROM A GROUP OF SONGS

1 In iTunes, click **Music**.

2 Press ⌘ and click any number of songs.

Note: You can press Shift and click a series of songs, all together.

3 Click **File**.

4 Click **New Playlist from Selection**.

iTunes creates a new playlist using the selected songs.

5 Type a new name for the playlist.

TIPS

How do I delete a song from a playlist?

You can delete a song or several songs from a playlist by clicking the playlist to select it and then pressing ⌘+clicking the individual song or songs to select them. Press Delete. iTunes removes the song or songs from the playlist but leaves them in your iTunes library.

Are playlists only for music?

No. You can build playlists that include songs, podcasts, audio books, videos, and links to Internet radio stations.

Smart playlists are a special kind of playlist with one or more features in common, such as the artist, style of music, or even a personal rating. You set the rules for the smart playlist, and iTunes updates them automatically. As you add new songs to the library, they appear in any smart playlists whose settings they match.

Create a Smart Playlist

① In iTunes, click **File**.

② Click **New Smart Playlist**.

The Smart Playlist dialog box appears.

*Note: Make sure that the **Match the following rule** check box is checked.*

③ Click the left 🔽 and select a criterion, such as **Artist**.

④ Click the middle 🔽 and select **is** (for the Artist criterion).

⑤ Click in the data field and type the qualifying criterion, such as an artist's name.

⑥ Click the Add button (⊕).

An additional set of search criteria appears.

● You can click here to select to match **Any** or **All** of the criteria that you set.

7 Repeat steps **3** to **5**, selecting other rules that you want to apply to the smart playlist.

● You can add additional sets of criteria by repeating steps **6** to **7**.

Note: You can have just one criteria apply to the rule as well, such as just the Folk genre.

8 Verify that **Live updating** is checked.

9 Click **OK**.

iTunes creates a smart playlist and fills it with any items in your list that match the criteria.

10 Type a name for your new smart playlist.

11 Press Return.

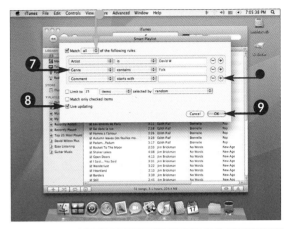

TIPS

What happens when I add new songs to the library?

Smart playlists are dynamic as long as the **Live updating** box is checked in the Smart Playlist dialog box. As you add items to the library matching a smart playlist's criteria, iTunes also adds the item to the smart playlist.

Do regular playlists get updated also?

No. You must update regular playlists manually when you add new content to the library and want it to be in a specific playlist.

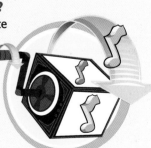

Browse Your Music Collection

You can browse and sort your music collection in various ways, such as by artist, by musical genre, or by album. You can also change the way that you view your collection and even view the album covers or other artwork. iTunes now includes an album artwork browser called *Cover Flow* for visually flipping through the album covers of music in your library.

Browse Your Music Collection

BROWSE YOUR COLLECTION BY GROUPING

1. In iTunes, click **Music**.

   The list of your music library appears.

2. Click **Artist**.

   The list is sorted alphabetically by each artist's first name.

Note: *You can sort by any other column heading by clicking it.*

3. Click the Browse button ().

   The Genre, Artist, and Album groupings appear at the top of the list.

4. Click the middle View button ( ).

● The album cover is displayed next to the songs in the list.

BROWSE YOUR COLLECTION WITH COVER FLOW

1 Click the right View button ().

Cover Flow displays the album covers.

2 Click and drag the scrollbar to browse your collection.

● To play a song, double-click the name when it appears highlighted below the artwork.

TIPS

How do I get the album cover to appear if I imported my own music CD?

iTunes can query the iTunes store for the music in your library and download the album art. Click a song in the list and click **Advanced**. Click **Get Album Artwork**. With an Internet connection, iTunes links to the iTunes store. You need to create an iTunes store account. iTunes searches its archives and, if it is available, downloads the album cover.

Can I also see the artwork for a video or other items?

Videos purchased from the iTunes store come with artwork. You can also add artwork to any items in your library. Click **View**. Click **Show Artwork** to open the Artwork viewer in the lower-left corner. Click a song or press ⌘+click multiple items in the list. In the Finder, navigate to and click and drag an image file, such as a JPEG, into the artwork viewer.

Favorite Movies

If your Macintosh has a CD or DVD burner, you can use iTunes to record, or *burn*, a music CD of your playlists and then play it in a separate CD player. If you plan to play the CD in a consumer CD player, use blank CD-R discs to burn your music. Although you can use other media with your Mac, most consumer CD players require CD-R media.

Burn a Music CD

① In iTunes, click the playlist that you want to burn as a music CD.

② Click here to select the numbered column for sorting.

③ Click and drag any songs to rearrange the order.

Note: *iTunes burns the songs on the audio CD in the order that you set.*

④ Click **iTunes**.

⑤ Click **Preferences**.

The iTunes Preferences window opens.

6 Click **Advanced**.

7 Click **Burning**.

The Burning Preferences pane appears with the name of your CD or DVD burner listed.

Note: *If you have more than one burner built in or have a compatible external CD/DVD burner connected to your Mac, select the burner to use from the CD Burner pop-up menu.*

8 Click **Audio CD** (○ changes to ◉).

Note: *You can change the time between songs and more in this window.*

9 Click **OK**.

10 Click **Burn Disc**.

● iTunes request a blank CD.

11 Insert a blank CD and click **Burn Disc** again.

iTunes burns the CD of your selected playlist.

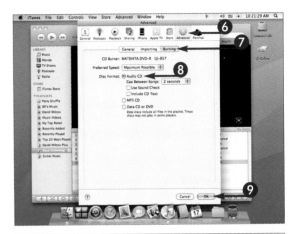

TIPS

What if my playlist has more songs than can fit on the CD?

iTunes will fill the first CD and then ask you to insert another blank disc.

Will the sound levels of all the songs match when I play back the CD?

To make sure that all the sound levels match, click **Use Sound Check** (☐ changes to ☑) in the Burning Preferences of the Advanced tab of the iTunes Preferences window.

Back Up Your iTunes Library

With iTunes included in Mac OS X Leopard, you can back up your entire iTunes library to CD or DVD. iTunes can even perform incremental backups, adding only new or updated items from your library each time. You can use these backup discs to restore your iTunes library.

Back Up Your iTunes Library

BURN A BACKUP DISC

① In iTunes, click **File**.

② Click **Back Up to Disc**.

The iTunes Backup dialog box appears.

③ Click **Back up entire iTunes library and playlists** (○ changes to ◉).

④ Click **Only back up items added or changed since last backup** (☐ changes to ☑).

⑤ Click **Back Up**.

● iTunes requests a blank disc.

6 Insert the blank disc.

The backup starts burning to disc.

RESTORE FROM A BACKUP DISC

1 Click 🎵.

2 Insert the backup disc.

A dialog box appears, asking if you want to restore from the disc.

3 Click **Restore**.

Note: *Click Overwrite existing files (☐ changes to ☑) to replace all existing files with the same name as those on the disc. Leave the box unchecked to place only files with different names into the library.*

The restoration of your library and playlists begins.

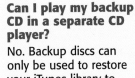

What kind of discs can I use to back up my library?

You can use CD-R, CD-RW, DV-R, DVD-RW, DVD+R, or DVD+RW discs to back up as long as you have the appropriate burner for the discs. And if your library is too large for one disc, a dialog box appears asking if you want to use multiple discs.

Can I play my backup CD in a separate CD player?

No. Backup discs can only be used to restore your iTunes library to iTunes. You cannot play these in a CD or DVD player.

iTunes makes it easy to print a CD case insert to match any playlist that you burned to CD. iTunes automatically formats the insert, and you can choose to print a number of different professional-looking album covers or only a text listing of the songs on the CD.

Print a CD Case Insert

1 In iTunes, click the playlist whose CD you want a CD case insert for.

● Click a song in the playlist if you want to use its art for the insert.

2 Click **File**.

3 Click **Print**.

The iTunes Print dialog box appears.

4 Click **CD jewel case insert** (○ changes to ⊙).

5 Click the Theme ⬍.

6 Click the type of CD case insert that you want, such as **Single Cover**.

For Single Cover, if you selected a song earlier, the album cover artwork from the selected song appears in the Preview window.

Note: You can also choose to print just a list of the songs or a mosaic of different album covers from the playlist.

7 Click **Print**.

The Print dialog box appears.

8 Click the Show More button ().

The dialog box enlarges.

9 Click to select different selections for your particular printer.

10 Click **Print**.

*Note: You can click **Preview** to see how the page will appear and then click **Print**.*

The CD case insert is printed.

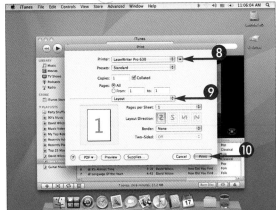

TIPS

How do I get album artwork or images onto my CD inserts?

If you purchased a song or CD from the iTunes store, the artwork is automatically downloaded, or you can check the iTunes store for album art for your own CD collection. You can also copy any image files into the artwork section in iTunes for any selected song.

Can I just print or save a list of the songs in my playlist?

In the iTunes Print dialog box, click **Song listing** (○ changes to ●). Click the Theme ⬦, click **Songs**, and click **Print**. In the following dialog box, click **Print** or click **PDF**. By clicking **PDF** and then clicking **Save as PDF**, you can save your list on your hard drive to use as a reference catalog for your playlists.

Share Music on a Network

You can listen to any music that you download or import into your own iTunes library. You can also share libraries with up to five computers over a local network, so others in your office or workgroup can listen to items from your library, and you can listen to their playlists. You can limit sharing to specific playlists and to specific people on your network.

Share Music on a Network

SHARE YOUR MUSIC

1 With iTunes open, click **iTunes**.

2 Click **Preferences**.

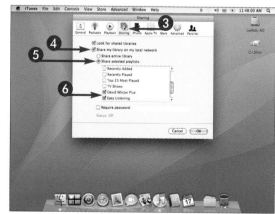

The iTunes Preferences window opens.

3 Click **Sharing**.

The Sharing settings appear.

4 Click **Share my library on my local network** (☐ changes to ☑).

5 Click **Share selected playlists** (○ changes to ◉).

6 Click the playlists to share (☐ changes to ☑).

⑦ Click **Require password** (☐ changes to ☑).

⑧ Type a password.

⑨ Click **OK**.

iTunes now only allows others on the network to listen to the selected playlists if they have the password.

LISTEN TO SHARED MUSIC

① Click a shared playlist in the iTunes list.

iTunes searches the network and displays the shared songs.

② Click a song.

③ Click ▶.

iTunes plays the selected song.

TIPS

How do I remove a shared playlist from my iTunes window?

You remove a shared playlist by clicking the Eject button (⏏) by the name of the playlist.

Can several people listen to my music at the same time?

Yes. Any number of people can share your music on your local network. However, for any songs purchased from the iTunes store, only five authorized computers can play those songs at one time. You can authorize a computer by entering the Apple ID and password of the person who purchased the songs when iTunes requests this information.

Search for Educational Podcasts and Videos

Podcasts are multimedia files that you download from the Internet to play on your computer or on an iPod. You can subscribe to a podcast so that it is automatically updated in your iTunes library when the author of the podcast adds more content. You can search for, download, and subscribe to many free educational and other podcasts from the iTunes store.

Search for Educational Podcasts and Videos

① Click ⬛.

iTunes launches.

② Click **iTunes Store**.

iTunes connects to the iTunes store through your Internet connection and displays the iTunes store in the window.

③ In the Quick Links section, click **Browse**.

The iTunes window changes to an organized list view.

④ Click **Podcasts**.

The Podcast list appears.

⑤ Click a category of interest in the Category list.

⑥ Click a subcategory in the Subcategory list.

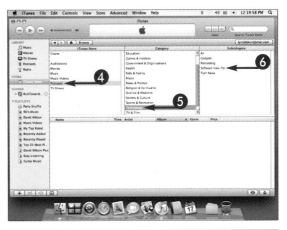

A list of available podcasts appears.

⑦ Click the podcast that you want to subscribe to.

⑧ Click **Subscribe**.

A dialog box appears, asking if you want to subscribe to download the current and all future episodes of the podcast.

⑨ Click **Subscribe**.

iTunes downloads and subscribes you to the podcast.

TIPS

Can I listen to or view a podcast without subscribing to it?

Yes. You can double-click any podcast in the list. iTunes downloads the podcast. When it is downloaded, the length of the podcast is listed in the Time column. Click ▶, and iTunes plays the podcast.

How do I view a podcast that includes video?

Double-click a downloaded podcast to start it. Click the Show Artwork button (▣) and click in the white artwork section. The video podcast window appears. You can resize the video podcast by clicking and dragging the lower-right corner of the window or by clicking **View** and clicking a different size, such as **Fit to Screen**.

Listen to Online Radio Stations

You can find and listen to a number of online radio stations from around the world using iTunes. Unlike podcasts, online radio stations continuously stream their content over the Internet. You can also save radio stations to a playlist so that you can easily access them later.

Listen to Online Radio Stations

LISTEN TO A RADIO STATION

① In iTunes, click **Radio**.

iTunes displays a list of radio categories.

② Double-click a category.

iTunes lists the available radio stations in the category.

③ Double-click a radio station.

iTunes downloads the stream for the radio station and begins playing.

SAVE A RADIO STATION TO A PLAYLIST

1 Click ⊞ under Playlists.

● A new playlist appears.

2 Type a name for your favorites radio playlist.

3 Click **Radio**.

4 Double-click a category.

5 Click and drag the radio station that you want to save into the new playlist.

The radio station is added to the playlist.

Note: You can add as many radio stations as you want to the playlist; however, you can only listen to radio stations in a playlist when you are connected to the Internet.

Can I save a song from the radio?

No. You can only save the radio station to a playlist.

Why do some of the radio stations have multiple entries in the category?

Some radio stations broadcast at different bit rates. If your Internet connection is slow or a radio station is not responding, click a station with a lower bit rate.

Working with Images and Video

You can purchase a variety of different applications to work with images and video on a Macintosh. Mac OS X Leopard, however, already includes basic software applications to enable you to import, view, edit, and have fun with images and video right away. These bundled applications are simple and easy to use.

Transfer Images to Your Computer

Most cameras come with separate image applications that you can install; however, Mac OS X Leopard includes an easy-to-use application called *Image Capture* for transferring images from your digital camera or scanner connected by USB, FireWire, or Bluetooth. With Image Capture, you can also transfer video clips and MP3 sounds from your camera to your Macintosh computer.

If your Mac has iPhoto installed, iPhoto launches by default whenever a camera is connected. You can use iPhoto to transfer images or change this preference in the Image Capture Preferences.

Transfer Images to Your Computer

① Using the USB or FireWire cables that came with it, connect your camera to the computer and turn on the camera.

② Click ▣.

A Finder window appears.

③ Click **Applications**.

④ Double-click **Image Capture**.

The Image Capture application launches.

Optionally, you can click ▣ on the Finder window to close it.

⑤ Click **Download Some**.

● You can click **Download All** to automatically download all the images, video, and MP3 files on the camera.

The window displays the camera's images.

6 Press and hold ⌘ and click each image to download.

7 Click **Download**.

● Image Capture downloads the selected images and opens the folder where they have been transferred.

TIPS

Where does Image Capture place the images?

Image Capture transfers images to the Pictures folder, video files to the Movies folder, and MP3 files to the Music folder. You can change these default settings and select your own folders for transfers. In the Image Capture window, click the Download To ⬍. Click **Other**. Navigate to and select a different folder and click **Open.**

What else can I do with Image Capture?

Image Capture enables you to rotate images for proper viewing and change an image's color profile. Depending on the camera model, you can share images over a local network and use Image Capture to transfer images, sounds, and videos from the computer to the camera. You can use Image Capture to set the date and time on some cameras. You can also use Image Capture with many scanners.

Preview Images Quickly

Preview is Mac OS X Leopard's simple yet convenient application for viewing images. Use Preview to take a quick look at photos and other images without launching other more-complicated applications. You can view a number of images within one Preview window.

Preview Images Quickly

① Click 📷.

A Finder window opens.

② Click **Applications**.

③ Double-click **Preview**.

The Preview application launches.

Optionally, you can click 🔘 on the Finder window to close it.

④ Click **File**.

⑤ Click **Open**.

An Open dialog box appears.

⑥ Navigate to a folder of image files.

⑦ Press and hold ⌘ and click all the images to open.

⑧ Click **Open**.

Note: *You can open just one photo by double-clicking its name.*

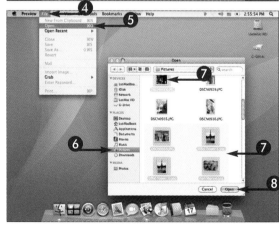

The first image opens in the main Preview window, and the others appear in the sidebar.

9 Click and drag the slider to the right to see larger previews in the sidebar.

10 Click an image to rotate.

The image appears in the main Preview window.

11 Click **Tools**.

12 Click **Rotate Left** or **Rotate Right** depending on your photo.

The photo rotates in the selected direction.

13 Repeat step **12** if necessary.

 TIPS

What kinds of image file types can I open in Preview?

Preview can open most of the different image file formats, including JPG, TIF, PNG, PSD, GIF, and even some proprietary camera manufacturers' RAW formats, including Canon's CR2 files and Nikon's NEF files.

Can Preview open other kinds of files?

Yes. Preview can open PDFs and animated GIF files. You can also use Preview to annotate and print PDFs without opening another application.

Convert Images to Different Formats

You can use Preview to convert an image to a different file format. Changing file formats can be useful for reducing the file size before sending photos with email or opening images in an application that cannot read the image's existing file type.

Convert Images to Different Formats

① Open the image or images that you want to convert in Preview.

Note: See the previous section, "Preview Images Quickly," to open one or more images in Preview.

② Click **File**.

③ Click **Save As**.

A dialog box appears.

④ Type a name in the Save As data field.

⑤ Click 🔽 to expand the dialog box.

6 Click a location to save the converted file type.

7 Click the Format ⟂ and select the new file type.

Note: If you select JPEG, you have the option of reducing the quality to reduce the file size for sending email attachments.

8 Click here to uncheck **Hide Extension** (☑ changes to ☐).

9 Click **Save**.

● Preview converts the file type, changes the name in the Preview window, and saves the file in the designated location.

TIPS

What if I just want to change the name and not the file type of the photo?

You can use the Save As command in Preview to change the name of an image. Preview automatically makes a duplicate copy of the file and applies the new name.

Why are there so many image file formats?

Each format has a different purpose. Some formats, such as JPEG, are better than others for creating small photo files for sharing on the Internet or in email. Some formats such as GIF compress the data to a minimum number of colors to reduce size. Other formats do not compress the data, leaving the image more editable.

Apply Simple Effects to Photos

Using Mac OS X Leopard's Preview application, you can make basic adjustments and improve your digital images. Preview enables you to change the exposure and increase the sharpness of digital photos without opening other applications.

Apply Simple Effects to Photos

APPLY EFFECTS

① Open an image in Preview.

Note: See the section "Preview Images Quickly" for help if needed.

② Click **Tools**.

③ Click **Image Correction**.

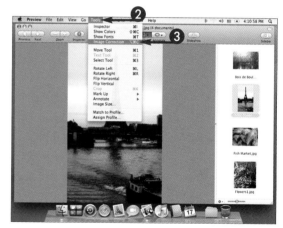

The Image Correction dialog box appears.

④ Click and drag the dialog box by its title bar so that you can see the photo.

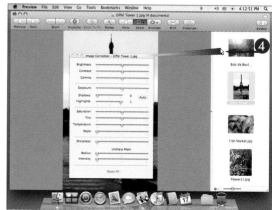

⑤ Click and drag the Exposure in either direction.

⑥ Click and drag the Sharpness in either direction.

⑦ Click and drag other s to apply their effects.

● You can click **Reset All** to revert the image to the original if you do not like the changes.

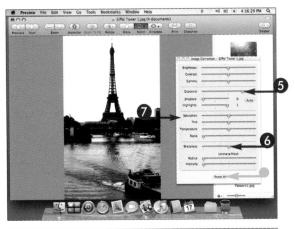

APPLY A SEPIA TONE

⑧ Click and drag the Sepia to the right.

The image turns sepia colored.

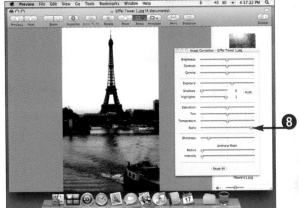

TIP

How can I tell if my changes really improve the final image?

Preview is useful for quick enhancements to photos when you do not have a refined image-editing application such as Adobe Photoshop. You should view your images at full or actual size to judge the exposure corrections and especially the sharpness. To preview your photo at actual size, click **View → Actual Size**. Click the Move tool and click and drag in your photo to move the image around on the screen and look at each area carefully. Then click **View → Zoom To Fit** to fit the entire photo onscreen and see the overall corrections. Always remember, your monitor quality and calibration is most important when viewing photos.

One of the easiest ways to view a series of images is to use the slideshow capabilities in Preview. You can open a series of photos in Preview and add and delete photos from the slideshow.

Watch a Slideshow with Preview

WATCH A SLIDESHOW

1 Open the images that you want in the slideshow in Preview.

***Note:** See the section "Preview Images Quickly" for help if needed.*

The Preview window shows the first image, and the others appear in the sidebar.

2 Click **View**.

3 Click **Slideshow**.

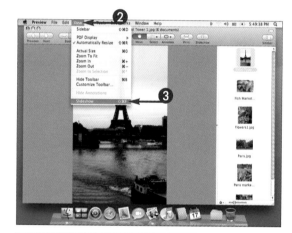

The screen turns black and plays a slideshow of the images in the Preview sidebar.

4 Click the Slideshow Close button (⊗) to return to the Preview screen.

REMOVE AN IMAGE FROM THE SLIDESHOW

1 Click the image to remove in the sidebar.

2 Click **Edit**.

3 Click **Cut**.

The image is removed from the slideshow but not from the folder where it is stored.

ADD AN IMAGE TO THE SLIDESHOW

1 Click to open a Finder window.

2 Navigate to the folder with the photo to add.

3 Click and drag the photo to the sidebar of the Preview window.

● A colored line indicates where the added photo will be placed in the slideshow order.

TIPS

Are there any keyboard shortcuts to use with a slideshow?

Yes. Pressing Esc stops the slideshow and returns you to the normal screen view, just like clicking ⊗. You also can press Spacebar to stop or start the slideshow. Move the cursor over the bottom of the image to view the control strip.

Can I see more than one photo at once?

Yes. You can view multiple images as an index sheet on a black background by clicking the Index Sheet button (⊞) on the control strip.

Take a Quick Look at an Image with the QuickTime Player

In addition to playing audio files, the QuickTime Player bundled with Mac OS X Leopard can be used as a quick way to view a still image.

Take a Quick Look at an Image with the QuickTime Player

1 In the Finder, press ⌘+A.

The Applications window appears.

2 Press Q and navigate to the QuickTime application.

3 Press Option and double-click the QuickTime Player icon.

The QuickTime Player opens, and the Applications window closes.

Optionally, you can click ⊗ to close the QuickTime Player window.

4 Click **File**.

5 Click **Open File**.

The Open dialog box appears.

6 Navigate to the location of the image file that you want to view.

7 Click the image file.

8 Click **Open**.

The image appears at actual size in the QuickTime Player window.

⑨ Click **View**.

⑩ Click **Enter Full Screen**.

The QuickTime Player window resizes to fill the screen with a black border.

TIPS

What types of files can I open with the QuickTime Player?

QuickTime can open BMP, GIF, JPEG/JFIF, JPEG 2000, PDF, MacPaint, PICT, PNG, Photoshop (PSD), SGI, Targa, FlashPix, and TIFF still images.

Can I view animated GIF files in the QuickTime Player?

Yes. The QuickTime Player can display animated graphics in a number of formats, including GIF, FLC, Flash, and PICS. Open an animated GIF file as you would any still image file.

Watch Movies with the QuickTime Player

The QuickTime Player is a multipurpose multimedia player. Not only can you use the QuickTime Player to display still images and play music files, but you can also use it to watch movies from your computer's hard drive or on a CD and even some movie file types on DVD. For many video files, the QuickTime Player enables you to control the sound and the playback.

Watch Movies with the QuickTime Player

PLAY A MOVIE

① Open the QuickTime Player as shown in the previous section.

② Click **File**.

③ Click **Open File**.

The Open dialog box appears.

④ Navigate to the location of the movie file that you want to view.

⑤ Click the movie file.

⑥ Click **Open**.

Note: If the movie is on a CD or DVD in the disc drive, you can double-click the disc icon and navigate to the movie file.

A QuickTime window appears.

⑦ Click the Play button (▶).

The movie starts playing.

⑧ Click the Pause playback button (⏸) to pause the movie.

CONTROL THE PLAYBACK

① With the movie open in the QuickTime window, click **Window**.

② Click **Show A/V Controls**.

The A/V Controls window opens.

③ Click ▶.

The movie starts playing.

④ Click and drag any of the sliders to change the audio or video playback.

Can I make a movie play repeatedly?

Yes. You can click **View →** **Loop**. Each time the movie ends, it will automatically start again at the beginning until you either click ❙❙ or press Spacebar. You can also press ⌘+L to turn on and off looping.

What is QuickTime Pro?

QuickTime Pro is an advanced version of QuickTime. You can purchase a QuickTime Pro license code by clicking **QuickTime Player → Buy QuickTime Pro** using an Internet connection. QuickTime Pro adds more capabilities to your current QuickTime application, including playing movies in Full Screen mode; editing and recording audio and video; adding special effects; and converting video, audio, and images to different formats.

If your Macintosh has a DVD drive, you can watch DVD movies on your computer. You can resize the window so that you can watch the movie while you work on other projects. You can also set the built-in DVD Player to open automatically when a DVD is inserted and have the movie fill the screen to improve the experience.

Watch Movies with the DVD Player

WATCH A DVD MOVIE

① Click .

A Finder window appears.

② Click **Applications**.

③ Press Option and double-click **DVD Player**.

The Finder window closes, and the DVD Player window appears with a floating control panel below it.

④ Click **View**.

⑤ Click **Enter Full Screen**.

The DVD window fills the screen.

⑥ Insert the DVD.

The DVD loads and plays in the DVD window.

● Optionally, you can press ⌘+K to open the Video Zoom box and click **Auto Zoom** to remove letterboxing.

WATCH A DVD MOVIE IN FULL SCREEN MODE AUTOMATICALLY

① Perform the preceding steps **1** to **3** to open the DVD Player.

② Click **DVD Player**.

③ Click **Preferences**.

The DVD Player Preferences window appears.

④ Click **Player**.

⑤ Make sure that both check boxes for **When DVD Player opens** are selected.

⑥ Click **OK**.

⑦ Press ⌘+Q.

The DVD Player application quits.

⑧ Insert a DVD.

The DVD Player launches and automatically fills the screen with the movie.

 TIPS

How can I get back to the Finder when I am watching a movie in Full Screen mode?

Press ⌘+F anytime to toggle between Full Screen mode and the Window mode with the Finder viewable. You can keep watching the movie while you change viewing modes.

How can I control the movie when I am watching in Full Screen mode?

If you move the mouse pointer over the bottom of the screen, the control panel appears there. If you move the mouse pointer over the top of the screen, the DVD Player menu appears along with the chapter, bookmark, and video clip listings. You can also press Spacebar to pause and restart the movie.

Have Fun Using Photo Booth

Leopard includes Apple's Photo Booth application. With an iSight or other video camera attached to your Mac, you can take quick snapshots of a subject in front of your screen. You can add a variety of visual effects and share the photos via email. You can even add Photo Booth effects live during a video iChat.

Have Fun Using Photo Booth

① Click ▦.

A Finder window appears.

② Click **Applications**.

③ Press Option and double-click **Photo Booth**.

The Finder window closes, and the Photo Booth window appears.

④ Click **Effects**.

The Photo Booth window fills with nine different photo effects.

5 Click the Forward arrow () or Back arrow (◄) to see different effects.

Note: The central photo is the Normal one in all sets.

6 Click an effect to select it.

The selected photo effect appears in the window.

7 Click the Photo button (📷) to take a photo with that effect.

● The photo appears in the Photo Well.

Optionally, repeat steps **5** to **7** to add more photos.

TIPS

Can I attach a Photo Booth photo to an email?

Yes. When you click a photo in the Photo Well, icons for Email, iChat Buddy Picture, and other Photo Booth–related applications installed on your Mac appear in the control strip above the Photo Well. Click the Email icon to automatically launch Mail and attach the Photo Booth photo.

How do I use Photo Booth for a video chat?

Launch iChat. In the menu bar, click **Video → Show Video Effects**. Click any effect to select it. In the menu bar, click **Video → Video Preview**. A Preview window opens showing the Photo Booth effect that your iChat buddies will see.

Get More Creative with Other Applications

When you are ready to unleash your creativity, you can purchase and install a variety of other more-powerful and advanced graphics applications. You can use Apple applications, including the iLife suite and more, or third-party applications from Adobe, Corel, and others that offer many more options for taking, changing, and sharing photos and video.

Apple's iLife Suite

The iLife suite from Apple is a collection of easy-to-use software applications that includes iPhoto for editing photos and iMovie for editing movies (and other "i" applications). iDVD enables you to burn movies, photos, and music onto DVDs with professional results. Garage Band helps you create music, and iWeb demystifies the creation and publishing of Web sites.

Apple's Advanced Applications

Apple also makes a number of professional-level software applications. Aperture is an organizational editing tool for professional photographers. Final Cut Studio is a complete professional-level video production studio, and special effects can be added with Shake. Logic Pro is for professional-level music creation and production.

Adobe Photoshop

Adobe Photoshop has long been the standard for editing digital photos at the professional level. You can use Photoshop to edit and enhance photos with the ultimate control. With Photoshop, you can also completely alter the photographs, add text, create professional designs, and even change photographs into stylized or fine-art images. Adobe also makes Photoshop Lightroom, a new application to help serious photographers import, organize, and display large quantities of digital images.

Other Video Tools

Adobe and other manufacturers make additional professional-level software for editing and producing videos with the Macintosh operating system. In addition, Adobe and others make applications for designing and publishing Web pages, recording, editing and producing audio, and creating special cinematographic effects and animation.

Corel Painter

Corel Painter takes photo editing into the world of fine art, with digital paint tools that mimic real-world art media from charcoal to oil paint. With Corel Painter, you can turn your photos into art or create art from scratch.

10

Connecting to Other Machines over a Network

A network consists of two or more computers or computer devices communicating with each other. Networks are useful for sharing files with others, or for sharing a printer on the network, or just to communicate over any distance with others. With Mac OS X Leopard, you can create and use a computer network without being a computer guru.

Understanding Networks

Computer networks come with a whole new vocabulary of words and acronyms. Learning to use a network can seem intimidating. The Macintosh operating system actually does most of the work behind the scenes to make connecting to one computer or many computers and other devices much easier.

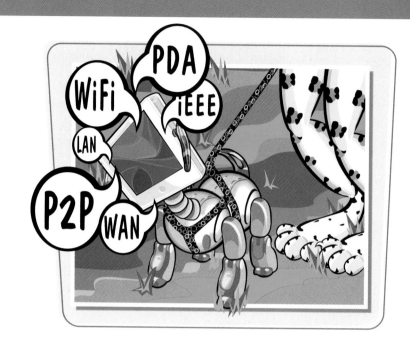

Types of Networks

A network can be as simple as a computer and a PDA or two computers connected with one cable in one room or as complex as thousands of computers covering a broad geographical area. Networks can be wired or wireless or can include a combination of both wired and wireless connections.

Common Networking Acronyms

Networks are often described by their size, such as a LAN (local area network) or a WAN (wide area network). The connection method, such as Ethernet cables (IEEE 802.3) or wireless (Wi-Fi or 802.11), or the relationship of the computers and devices, such as client/server or peer-to-peer (P2P) also describe different network types.

LANs and WANs

A LAN refers to computers within one local area, such as a home or office. Most LANs connect using Ethernet and Wi-Fi. A WAN covers a large geographical area, connecting many individual computers or LANs together to a larger network. The Internet is the largest WAN.

Your Computer's Name and Address

Each computer in a network has a name and address. You name the computer when you first set it up. The local hostname identifies machines on a local network. The IP (Internet protocol) address is a set of numbers assigned by the server as your location on the Internet.

Client/Server and Peer-to-Peer

Client/server and *peer-to-peer* are different types of network architecture. Client computers send requests for data to the server, which contains only databases and applications. A P2P network comprises multiple computers that act independently as both a client and a server.

About Passwords

Passwords protect your information for multiple users on one computer and over a network. You need a password to perform many tasks on the computer, to access shared folders on a network, and to access servers and certain Web sites.

Change Your Computer's Name

Other computers on the local network see your computer by its local hostname, the name followed by ".local." When you first set up your computer, you gave it a name. You can change the name using System Preferences.

1 Click .

2 Click **System Preferences**.

The System Preferences window appears.

3 Click **Sharing** in the Internet & Network section.

The Sharing Preferences pane opens.

④ Click and drag through the Computer Name data field.

The current name is highlighted.

⑤ Type a new computer name.

⑥ Press **Return**.

⑦ Click to close the window and quit System Preferences.

The computer name changes, along with the local hostname.

Note: *Changing the name of your computer does not change the name of your hard drive.*

TIPS

What is the local hostname?
The local hostname for your computer is your computer's address on the local network. It ends in ".local." Other users on the local network can use the local hostname to access files on your computer.

How can I prevent others on the network from seeing or accessing my computer?
Other computers on the local network can only see your computer if you have clicked **File Sharing** in the Service section of the Sharing Preferences window. They need a password to access files on your computer.

Understanding Passwords

Unlike other personal computers, Mac OS X Leopard is a secure computing environment. Mac OS X Leopard enables you to control access to various folders, preferences, accounts, and other resources on your computer using passwords. You can add and change passwords and store them in a keychain.

Different Types of Passwords

Depending on your computing environment, you may choose to use one or more different passwords with your computer. Mac OS X Leopard includes four different types of passwords: administrator passwords, user account passwords, a master password, and keychain passwords.

The Administrator Password

The administrator controls other users on the same computer. An administrator password is required to perform many systemwide tasks, such as setting System Preferences and installing software. An administrator account is created when you first set up Leopard on your computer.

Your User Account Password

When you create your user account, you assign a user account password so that you can log in to your individual Home folder. One computer can have multiple user accounts, each with a different password. You can change your user account password anytime you are logged in.

The Master Password

A master password can be set up by the administrator to work with the FileVault, a tool for locking and encrypting a user's Home folder. The master password is not the same as the user login password, adding a higher level of security.

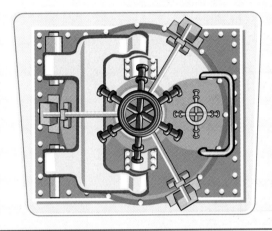

A Keychain

Each user can have a number of passwords for certain applications, Internet servers, Web sites, and shared folders. A keychain stores the various passwords for each user and can automatically fill in the information. The password for your main keychain is by default the same as your login password, but you can change it.

Adding Keychains

You can create an additional keychain to store information that you want kept confidential. Keychain Access is a small application in the Utilities folder. You can use it to create a new keychain and assign a password that is not automatically unlocked when you log in to your user account.

Change Your Password

You can change your account password anytime using System Preferences. If you are the administrator, you can change your account password as well as the password for other users on the computer.

Change Your Password

1 Click .

2 Click **System Preferences**.

The System Preferences window appears.

3 Click **Accounts** in the System section.

The Accounts Preferences pane opens.

④ Click your account.

⑤ Click **Change Password**.

A dialog box appears.

⑥ Click in the Old Password data field and type your old password.

⑦ Click in the New Password data field and type a new password.

⑧ Click in the Verify field and type the new password again.

⑨ Click in the Password Hint data field and type a hint for your password.

⑩ Click **Change Password**.

⑪ Click .

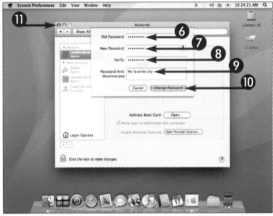

TIPS

What is 🔑 next to the New Password field for?

You click 🔑 to open the Password Assistant. The Password Assistant can help you select a new password, or if a password is already entered in the field, it indicates the level of security of your existing password.

What if I am the original administrator, and I forget my account password?

You can reset the original administrator account password by restarting from the Mac OS X Leopard Install DVD. When the Installer appears, click **Utilities → Reset Password**. Click the hard disk volume and select your original administrator's account name. Type a new password and click **Save**. Restart the computer again from the internal hard drive. You should change your login password in Keychain Access to match the new password.

Edit Network Settings

Networks at different locations, such as a work or school Ethernet network and your home network, require different settings. After creating separate locations in System Preferences as shown here, you can quickly switch connection settings when you change from one network to another by clicking ■ → Location to select a different network.

Edit Network Settings

① Click ■.

② Click **System Preferences**.

The System Preferences window appears.

③ Click **Network** in the Internet & Network section.

The Network pane opens.

④ Click the Location ⬍.

⑤ Click **Edit Locations**.

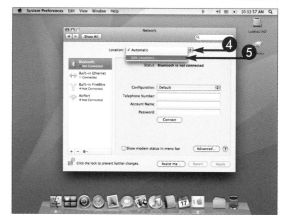

A dialog box appears.

6 Click ➕.

An untitled location appears highlighted.

7 Type a name for the new location.

8 Click **Done**.

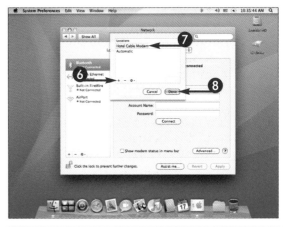

9 Click the type of network.

10 Click the Configure 🔽 to select the configuration according to your location.

Note: Your ISP provides the information for this section as explained in the Tip below.

11 Enter the settings for your new network location.

12 Click **Apply**.

Your new network location is created.

 TIP

How do I know what network settings to use?

Your Internet service provider (ISP) gives you the settings for your home network. The network administrator in an office or school location can help you set up a connection for an office or school network or access to the Internet. If you are in a hotel, the network settings are generally provided along with standard connection instructions on a card in the guest services book. You can also click **Assist Me** in the Network Settings Preferences pane, and Mac OS X Leopard guides you through the steps to set up a network connection, offering detailed instructions and descriptions for each step.

Set Up File Sharing

You can transfer files quickly with other computers on the network using file sharing. Each computer on the network must set up file sharing to be accessible to others. Place files to be shared in your Public folder, and other computers on the network can see and copy the files and also place files there to exchange with you.

Set Up File Sharing

SET UP FILE SHARING ON YOUR COMPUTER

1 Click ![Apple menu icon].

2 Click **System Preferences**.

The System Preferences window appears.

3 Click **Sharing** in the Internet & Network section.

The Sharing pane opens.

4 Click **File Sharing** (☐ changes to ☑) in the sidebar.

5 Click ![icon].

Your computer is now ready to share files on the local network.

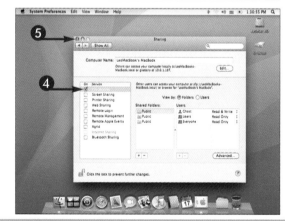

SHARE FILES IN YOUR PUBLIC FOLDER

① Click in the Dock.

A Finder window opens.

② Click your Home folder.

The Home folder's contents appear in the window.

③ Double-click the folder with the files that you want to share.

Note: You may need to press ⌘ as you double-click to open a second window depending on your Finder Preferences.

A second Finder window opens.

④ Click and drag the windows to see both at the same time.

⑤ Click and drag a file to share to move it into the Public folder.

Optionally, you can press Option as you click and drag the file to place a copy in the Public folder.

⑥ Repeat step **5** for all the files that you want to share.

The files are available to others on the network.

TIPS

Is there a way to share a file with someone who is not on a network?

Yes. You can use the so-called "sneaker net" method. You can copy the files from your computer onto removable media such as a CD or a flash drive and carry the media over to the other computer to plug it in and copy it to that machine.

Can someone on the network share files with me but keep others on the network from seeing the files?

Yes. You can use the Public folder's Drop Box folder to do so. Your friend or colleague on the network can copy files to your Drop Box, but no one but you can see their contents. When you open your Public folder on your computer, you can see the transferred files in your Drop Box.

Connect to Other Computers over a Local Network

Mac OS X Leopard enables you to connect to other computers on a local network. You can connect as a guest to access the Public folder or with a password for greater access. You can also connect to a Windows computer on the network, if the Windows computer has enabled certain folders for sharing.

You may share the labours of the great, but you may not share the spoil!

That's from "The Lion's Share" by Aesop!

Connect to Other Computers over a Local Network

① Click 🖥 in the Dock.

A Finder window opens.

② Click the **Network** folder.

The Network window appears, displaying the connected computers.

③ Double-click a networked computer's name.

● Another window appears, showing the folders on the networked computer and your connection as a guest.

Note: *A guest only has access to a Drop Box and only if the registered owner has set up permissions in the Get Info box.*

④ Click **Connect As**.

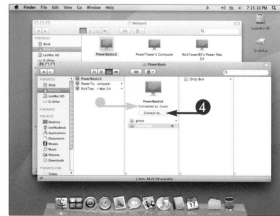

A dialog box appears with your own computer's name.

5 Click **Registered User** (⊙ changes to ⊙).

6 Click and drag through the Name field to highlight it.

7 Type the username for the networked computer.

8 Type the password for the registered user.

9 Click **Connect**.

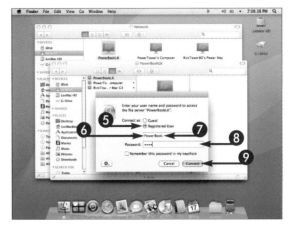

● The volumes on the networked computer appear and are accessible in the Finder window.

I know there is another Mac on my network, but it does not appear in the Network window. How can I connect to it?

Click **Go → Connect to Server**. Type the other computer's IP address in the Connect to Server dialog box and click **Connect**. You can find the IP address in the Sharing pane of the System Preferences on the other Mac. The address is listed at the top of the window when Personal File Sharing is turned on.

How can Windows users connect with my Macintosh?

In the Sharing pane of the System Preferences, click **Advanced**. Click **Share files and folders using SMB** (☐ changes to ☑) and click the account to share. Enter the account password in the Authenticate dialog box, click **OK**, and then click **Done**. The Windows user also needs the network address and a username and password for an account on your Macintosh.

Share a Printer

You can share a printer connected to your Mac with other computers on the local network. You must first turn on Printer Sharing in System Preferences. The shared printer appears in the Print dialog boxes of any other connected computers.

Share a Printer

① Click .

② Click **System Preferences**.

The System Preferences window appears.

③ Click **Print & Fax** in the Hardware section.

The Print & Fax Preferences pane appears.

④ Click a printer if there is more than one in the Printers list box.

⑤ Click **Share this printer** (☐ changes to ☑).

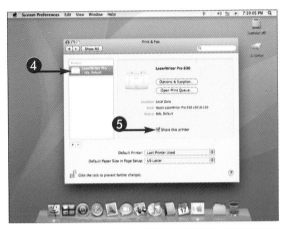

⑥ Click .

The printer is now accessible to other computers on your local network.

*Note: If you have more than one printer, you can click one or more printers' names in the sidebar and click **Share this printer** to make any or all of the printers accessible to other networked computers.*

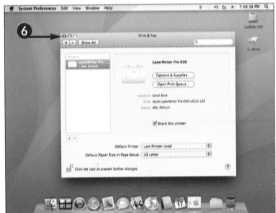

TIPS

Can I also set up Printer Sharing in the Internet & Network Preferences?

Yes. You can click **Sharing** in the Internet & Network section of System Preferences. In the Service list box, click **Printer Sharing** (☐ changes to ☑). This automatically checks the Printer Sharing box in the Print & Fax pane of the Hardware Preferences as well.

Does the shared printer print in a specific order?

The shared printer prints the files in the order that they are received in the queue. The computer to which the shared printer is physically attached becomes a host for the printer's queue.

Understanding a .Mac Account

A .Mac account is a membership-based suite of Internet services from Apple. The suite includes an email account, a Web-based storage area called *iDisk*, a fast way to synchronize your calendar and Address Book, and easy-to-use tools for sharing and communicating.

.Mac Mail

.Mac Mail has built-in virus protection and has no pop-up ads. You can use .Mac Mail with Mac OS X Leopard's email client called *Mail,* as well as others such as Outlook or Netscape, and check your .Mac email account from any computer with an Internet connection and a browser.

iDisk

A .Mac account includes your own special storage area on the Apple server. You can use your iDisk as a backup for valuable files, a place to access important files anytime from other computers, or an easy place to share with others by storing items in the iDisk Public folder.

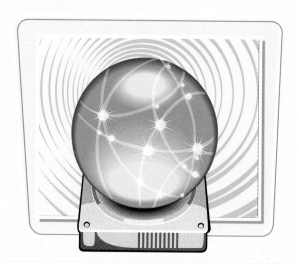

Synchronization

If you have more than one Macintosh or if you ever use another computer for Internet access, a .Mac account becomes even more valuable. With .Mac Sync, you can keep your iCal calendars, Address Book contacts, and Safari bookmarks the same on all your Macs. You can also access these from any other computer with an Internet connection, including PCs.

.Mac Group

If you manage a club or group or you regularly exchange files with friends, the Groups feature of a .Mac account offers more advantages, such as a group email address and a private, password-protected Web site for publishing group photos or managing the group's calendar of events.

Online Sharing

A .Mac membership enables you to communicate creatively without learning any applications. You can create custom iCards with photos and artwork to send through email and use the HomePage tool to quickly create a variety of different styled Web pages and publish them to the Web.

Set Up iChat

iChat in Mac OS X Leopard brings Mac simplicity to instant messaging and audio and video conferencing, making it easy to stay in touch with individuals or groups over any distance. With an Internet connection and either a .Mac, AOL, AIM, or Jabber screen name, you can set up iChat instant messaging and then add buddies to your iChat list.

Set Up iChat

SET UP YOUR ICHAT ACCOUNT

1 Click the iChat icon ( ) in the Dock.

The iChat Setup Assistant window appears.

2 Click **Continue**.

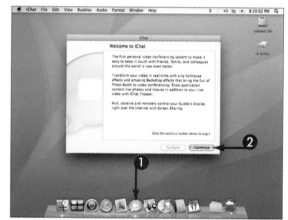

3 Click and select **.Mac Account** or **AIM Account**.

4 Click here and type your screen name or .Mac member name.

5 Click here and type your password.

● You can click **Get an iChat Account** instead to go to the .Mac sign-up page.

6 Click **Continue**.

7 Click **Continue** in all the following windows.

8 Click **Done**.

A window appears, confirming that iChat is set up.

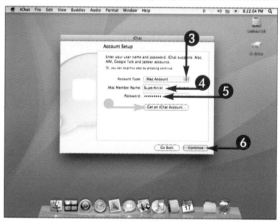

ADD A BUDDY TO YOUR ICHAT LIST

1 Click .

iChat launches, and a Buddy List appears on the screen.

2 Click **Buddies**.

3 Click **Add Buddy**.

A dialog box appears.

4 Type your buddy's account or screen name.

5 Click ⊞ to change **AIM** to **.Mac** if necessary.

6 Type the buddy's first and last names in the fields.

7 Click **Add**.

Your new buddy now appears on your Buddy List.

TIPS

How do I add a buddy directly from my Address Book?

Click **Buddies** → **Add Buddy**. In the dialog box, click ⊞ to open a small version of your Address Book. Click a name with an AIM or .Mac account and click **Add**.

Is there a benefit to using a .Mac account with iChat?

Yes. .Mac members can send instant messages, conduct audio or video chats, and even send files securely with 128-bit encryption. You can set up encryption in the Accounts window of the iChat Preferences. Click the **Security** tab and click **Encrypt**.

Send and Receive a File with iChat

iChat enables you to do much more than send and receive instant messages. You can send and receive files such as photos, and you can save any received files to your hard drive. With a microphone attached, you can also conduct an audio iChat. With a video or iSight camera, you can have a video chat and even add special effects.

Send and Receive a File with iChat

SEND A FILE WITH ICHAT

① In iChat, double-click the name of an available buddy in your Buddy List.

A Chat window appears.

② Type a message in the message field.

③ Click ☑ in the Dock.

④ Navigate to the folder with the file that you want to send.

⑤ Click and drag the file into the message field.

⑥ Press Return.

A window appears, saying the file is being sent and that iChat is waiting for your buddy to accept the file.

CHANGE THE LOCATION FOR DOWNLOADING RECEIVED ICHAT FILES

1 Click **iChat**.

2 Click **Preferences**.

The iChat Preferences window appears.

3 Click **General**.

4 Click the Save Received Files To ⟂ and select **Other**.

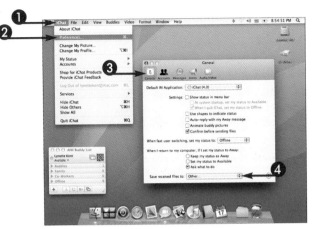

A dialog box drops down inside the Preferences window.

5 Navigate to and click another location to save the iChat files.

6 Click **Select**.

7 Click ⊙ to close the iChat Preferences window.

When you receive a file attached to an iChat message, click **Save File** in the Incoming File Transfer window to automatically download the file to the new location.

TIPS

What else can I do with iChat?

You can launch an audio or video chat by clicking the icons in the Buddy List. You can share your screen or a buddy's screen as you talk to easily collaborate on projects. To do so, click **Buddies → Share My Screen**. iChat starts the audio chat, and when your buddy accepts, he can see your screen on his display. You can even record your audio and video chats.

Can I change the background for a video chat?

Yes. You can drag any included iChat backdrop or drag your own photo or video into the iChat video window to make it look like you are chatting from a different location. You can also add Photo Booth effects to your image as you chat by clicking **Video** and clicking **Show Video Effects**.

CHAPTER 11

Simplifying Tasks and Maintenance

Mac OS X Leopard includes a number of useful applications and assistants to help you with everyday projects and to maintain your Mac. Whether you need to keep an address handy with a sticky note, find a lost password, or prepare an external hard drive to use as a backup, Leopard's bundled utilities and applications simplify every task.

Start with Good Mac Habits

Your Mac, like any tool or a car, will run better if you regularly follow good maintenance habits. You can avoid many problems or recover more easily from problems that do occur when you use certain tools and follow maintenance guidelines.

Keep Mac OS Software Up-to-Date

Keeping your Mac OS software up-to-date is the first step in Mac maintenance. Apple regularly publishes patches and bug fixes and adds new features to each version of the Mac OS X software after it is released. These incremental updates are numbered after a second decimal point, such as 10.5.1, 10.5.2, and should be downloaded and installed.

Keep Other Software Up-to-Date

Updates for other Apple software, such as iPhoto or iTunes, are listed in the Software Update window along with system software updates. Many third-party applications also have options for automatic updates and patches. You should regularly check the Web sites for your most-used software to download and install the updated versions.

Back Up Your Files

Your files are the most valuable part of your computer. Hard drive problems can be fixed or stolen computers can be replaced. You should back up your files, photographs, music collections, tax records, and more on separate hard drives, DVDs, or a network disk such as an iDisk for safekeeping. Use Leopard's Time Machine feature to simplify the backup process and make duplicate backups of your most important files.

Install Antivirus Software

Although Macs are not plagued like Windows computers with viruses and spyware, installing antivirus software can be a valuable tool in preventing problems. Intego's VirusBarrier, from Intego.com, is one of the most-used virus-protection software applications available and is easily updated automatically.

Use a Surge Suppressor or UPS

An electric surge, a brownout, or a blackout can burn computer circuits or cause hard drive failure. Always use a surge suppressor or, better still, an uninterruptible power supply (UPS). A UPS has a battery backup, so you can save open files and shut down properly during a power loss, protecting your equipment and your work.

Update Your Mac OS Software

Apple often releases minor updates to each major version of the system software — not only to fix any errors but also to introduce useful new features. By keeping your Mac OS software up-to-date, you can avoid potential problems and also take advantage of the newest additions. Leopard's Software Update feature does most of the work for you.

Update Your Mac OS Software

CONFIGURE SOFTWARE UPDATE

1 Click 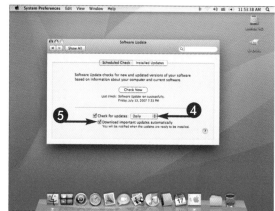.

2 Click **System Preferences**.

The System Preferences window appears.

3 Click **Software Update** in the System section.

The Software Update Preferences pane appears.

4 Click 🔁 and select **Daily**.

*Note: Click **Weekly** if you have a dial-up connection to save dial-up time.*

5 Click **Download important updates automatically** (🔲 changes to ✅).

RUN A SOFTWARE UPDATE CHECK

1 Perform the previous steps **1** to **3**.

2 Click **Check Now**.

● Software Update checks for new software over the Internet.

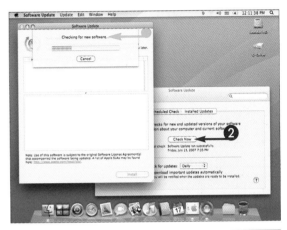

New software is listed in the window.

3 Click the items that you want to install (☐ changes to ☑).

4 Click **Install Number Items**.

Note: Items with ⊙ mean a restart will be required.

Software Update downloads and installs the selected items.

5 Click ⊙ to close the Software Update Preferences pane.

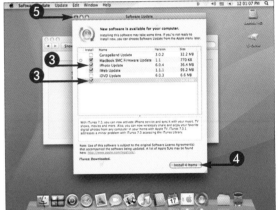

TIPS

Do I have to install the updates when they are downloaded?

No. You can install updates when you are ready. Click → **Software Update**. The Software Update window displays a list of any new updates, including those it has already downloaded but not yet installed. Click **Install Number Items**.

Are you ready to install now?

Should I check the boxes for items in the list that are not automatically checked and install these items?

Software Update lists all the new items that are available. Some items may not apply to your computer — for example, an AirPort update when you do not have an AirPort card installed. You can ignore these items.

Find a Lost Password

Filling out forms on Web pages, connecting to different networks, and even some applications require passwords. Over time, you will have many passwords on your system. You can find a lost password using the Keychain Access application included in Leopard's Utilities folder.

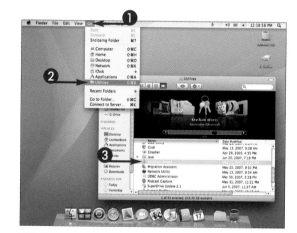

① Click **Go**.

② Click **Utilities**.

The Utilities folder window appears.

③ Press [Option] and double-click **Keychain Access**.

The Keychain Access window appears, and the Utilities window closes.

④ Click **Passwords**.

⑤ Double-click the item for which you have lost your password.

The Attributes pane of the information window for the selected item appears.

6 Click **Show password** (☐ changes to ☑).

A dialog box appears.

7 Type your keychain password.

Note: *Your keychain password is the same as your user account login password.*

Note: *An administrator can reset lost user account passwords. To reset a lost administrator account, you will have to restart from the Mac OS X DVD as described in Chapter 10.*

8 Click **Allow**.

The Attributes window shows the password for the item.

Can I change a password in Keychain Access?

Yes. You can change a password by double-clicking the password shown. Type a new password and click **Save Changes**.

Can I delete an item from a keychain if I do not use the item anymore?

Yes. You can delete an item, such as an Internet account that you no longer use, and remove a password from the list so that it is no longer stored in the keychain. Click the item to select it. In the menu bar, click **Edit → Delete**.

Monitor Your Computer's Activity

Using graphics or digital video applications or keeping multiple applications open taxes your computer's resources. The Activity Monitor displays your Mac's vital statistics, so you can view how or where your processor, RAM, and hard disk space are being used. It can alert you to potential problems and enable you to quit some applications, making the computer run more efficiently.

Monitor Your Computer's Activity

① In the Finder, click **Go**.

② Click **Utilities**.

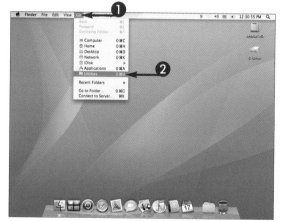

The Utilities window opens.

③ Press `Option` and double-click **Activity Monitor**.

The Utilities window closes, and the Activity Monitor window appears, displaying the open applications, running processes, and memory consumption.

④ Click **CPU**.

⑤ Double-click the CPU Usage graph.

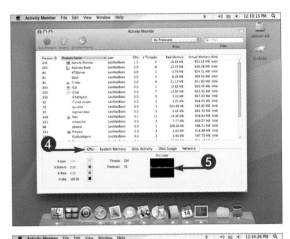

A small window opens showing the number of processors in your Mac with graphs monitoring usage in real time.

Note: *Apple Tech support may ask you to launch the Activity Monitor to help diagnose a problem.*

 TIPS

If one application is using almost 100% of the memory or CPU, what can I do?

If one application is hogging too much of the CPU or RAM, your processor may be overloaded or working slowly. You can quit the application by selecting it in the Activity Monitor window and clicking the **Quit Process** button. Click **Quit** in the confirmation dialog box that appears.

Can I just keep an eye on the memory usage?

Yes. You can keep an icon in the Dock to display the memory usage or another activity. Click and hold the Activity Monitor icon (🖼) in the Dock. Move the cursor in the contextual menu to **Dock Icon** and then to **Show Memory Usage** and release the mouse button. The memory usage is displayed in the Dock until you quit the Activity Monitor.

Check Your S.M.A.R.T. Status

You can avoid losing valuable information by checking the health of your internal hard disk on a regular basis. Most internal ATA drives include a built-in monitoring system called Self-Monitoring Analysis and Reporting Technology, or S.M.A.R.T. Use Mac OS X Leopard's Disk Utility to quickly check your S.M.A.R.T. status.

Check Your S.M.A.R.T. Status

① In the Finder, click **Go**.

② Click **Utilities**.

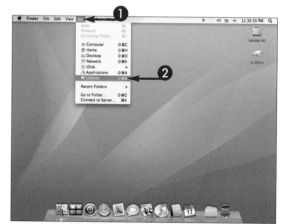

The Utilities window opens.

③ Press Option and double-click **Disk Utility**.

The Disk Utility window appears, and the Utilities window closes.

④ Click your hard drive in the list.

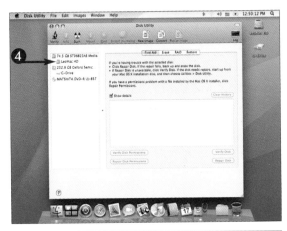

The bottom of the window displays information about the hard disk.

⑤ Look at the S.M.A.R.T. status on the bottom right.

● If the S.M.A.R.T. status shows **Verified**, your hard disk is OK.

How does the S.M.A.R.T. status let me know if my hard disk has a problem?

If the S.M.A.R.T. status shows **About to Fail** in red letters, your hard drive is in imminent danger of failing. Back up the hard drive or copy all your valuable data to another drive immediately. About to Fail indicates that the drive probably cannot be repaired with repair software, so you should replace it.

What kind of backup is best in case of a hard drive failure?

A bootable duplicate of your entire hard disk on an external hard drive, such as a G-Technology drive, enables you to recover almost immediately without losing any files. The type of external hard drive that you can use for such a backup depends on your Mac.

Clean Up Your Desktop

Adding files and folders on your desktop is similar to throwing stacks of papers on your desk. A cluttered desktop is prone to accidental mouse clicks and the unintentional opening or deleting of files. You can use smart folders with specific search criteria to organize your most often-used files so that they will be kept off your desktop but still easily accessible from any Finder window.

Clean Up Your Desktop

COLOR-CODE FILES TO ADD TO A SMART FOLDER

1 Press ⌘ and click the items to be grouped.

2 Click **File**.

3 Click a label color square for all the files.

The color is added to the name of all the files.

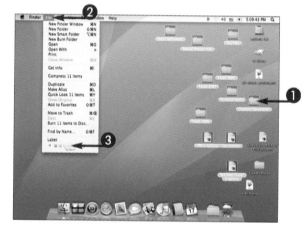

4 Click ⧉ to open a Finder window.

5 Click and drag the selected files into the Documents folder.

CREATE A NEW SMART FOLDER FOR THE COLOR-CODED FILES

① In a Finder window, click ✱▾.

② Click **New Smart Folder**.

A New Smart Folder Finder window appears.

③ Click ⊕.

The window expands.

④ Click **What** and select **Other**.

TIPS

How can I remove a smart folder from the Finder window sidebar?

You can click and drag the folder out of the sidebar area and release the mouse button. The folder disappears in a puff of smoke.

Does removing a smart folder from the sidebar remove it from my computer?

No. The smart folder is still located in the Documents folder or wherever you saved it. To remove the folder entirely, you can click and drag it from the Documents folder into the Trash.

continued

Smart folders use Spotlight searching to organize files regardless of where they are stored on your hard drive. Using smart folders, you can organize your files by what they share in common, such as the files used for one project or files modified on the same date.

A search attributes dialog box appears.

5 Click and drag here to scroll the list.

6 Click **File label** (☐ changes to ☑).

7 Click **OK**.

The file label criteria is added.

8 Click the same color that you did in step **3** of the first part of this task.

● You can click the ⊕ again to add more criteria to the smart folder.

9 Click **Save**.

A dialog box appears.

⑩ Click in this field and type a name for the smart folder.

⑪ Click the Where ⊡ and select a location.

⑫ Make sure that **Add To Sidebar** is checked.

⑬ Click **Save**.

● A new smart folder with a gear icon is added to the Finder window.

● All documents with the designated color are automatically added to the smart folder.

TIPS

What other types of search criteria can I use for smart folders?

You can group files by label, date, kind, content, keywords, creators, copyright, and more. You can also use multiple search criteria for one smart folder.

Can I keep one file in several smart folders?

Yes. You can have one file appear in multiple smart folders even though the file only exists in one location on your hard drive. A photo, for example, can appear in a smart folder of a vacation trip and a smart folder of files modified on a specific date.

Make Notes with Stickies

The Stickies application in Mac OS X Leopard acts just like paper sticky notes, so you can keep reminders to yourself or frequently used text available at all times on your computer screen. You can create new notes anytime — even while in another application, and you can use any selected text.

Make Notes with Stickies

MAKE A NEW STICKY NOTE

1. In the Finder, click **Finder**.

2. Click **Services**.

3. Click **Make New Sticky Note**.

Note: You can also press ⌘ + Shift + Y to open the Stickies application.

● If this is the first time that you are launching Stickies, the default notes appear. You can close these by clicking the top-left corner button on each note.

4. Click in the note and type the text of your note.

● You can click and drag the note to a different part of your screen.

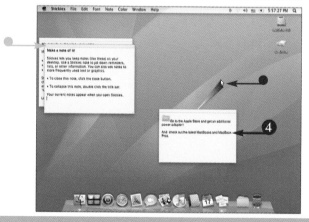

MAKE A STICKY NOTE FROM AN ADDRESS BOOK CARD

① Click the Address Book icon ( ) in the Dock.

The Address Book opens.

② Click the name of the contact whose information you want to place on a sticky note.

③ Click and drag through the text to save.

④ Click **Address Book**.

⑤ Click **Services**.

⑥ Click **Make New Sticky Note**.

● A new sticky note appears with the selected text.

Note: *You can create a sticky note using text from many applications by clicking* **Services** *in the application's menu.*

Can I change the sticky note color?

Yes. You can change the note color by clicking **Color** in the menu bar and clicking a different color. You can also format the text using different fonts, font sizes, and bold and italic text and can change the font color by clicking **Font** in the menu bar and clicking **Show Fonts** and **Show Colors** to open the editing palettes.

If I close the Stickies application, do I lose my notes?

No. Your notes will reappear when you again launch the Stickies application. You can delete a note by pressing ⌘ + W to close it and clicking **Don't Save**. If you close a note and click **Save**, you can save the sticky note's content as a text document on your computer.

Access and Customize Dashboard Utilities

The Dashboard is a convenient collection of handy utilities called *widgets*. Widgets are mini-applications that help with everyday tasks or provide quick information. You can access the Dashboard widgets easily and can customize the Dashboard to show the widgets that you want to see. You can also customize individual widgets.

Access and Customize Dashboard Utilities

① Click the Finder icon (⬜) in the Dock.

A Finder window appears.

② Click **Applications**.

③ Press Option and click Dashboard.

The Dashboard displaying several widgets appears as a semitransparent layer on the screen, and the Applications window closes.

④ Click ⊕.

A selection of widgets appears organized alphabetically in a row across the bottom of the screen.

⑤ Click ➡.

The row advances.

⑥ Click a widget.

The widget appears in the center of the Dashboard.

Note: *You can click and drag the widgets around the Dashboard.*

7 Click the **i** in the bottom-right corner of the widget.

The widget turns around to display customizable information.

● For the Stocks widget, you can type a stock symbol into the data field and press **Return** to add stock data to the list.

8 Click **Done**.

For the Stocks widget, the widget turns back around with the new stock symbol added to the list.

Note: *Different widgets have different controls and options.*

9 Click anywhere on the desktop.

The Dashboard closes.

TIPS

Can I have two of the same widget?
Yes. You may need two world clocks to instantly see the time in several time zones, or if you are going on a trip, you can set up two or more weather widgets, each listing the weather for a different area on your trip. Click the widget in the row to add a duplicate.

Are there keyboard shortcuts for the Dashboard?
Yes. You can press **F12** to open the Dashboard. You can change this key command or set the Dashboard to open when you hover the cursor over a screen corner using the Exposé & Spaces pane of the System Preferences window. Pressing **Option** and moving the cursor over a widget activates the Close button (⊗). Click the Close button to close a widget.

Create Your Own Web Widgets

With Mac OS X Leopard, you can create your own widgets without learning any computer code. You can create and customize a Web clip widget from any Web page so that you can quickly access your favorite sites. Click any links in your custom widget, and Safari opens the original Web site. You can create as many widgets as you want.

Create Your Own Web Widgets

① Click .

A Safari window opens.

② Type a URL in the Address field to open a favorite page.

③ Click the Open in Dashboard button (▦).

A highlighted rectangle appears on the darkened Safari window.

④ Move the cursor to move the rectangle over the specific area you want for the widget.

⑤ Click in the highlighted rectangle.

Corner and side anchors appears on the rectangle.

⑥ Click and drag the anchors to resize the rectangle.

⑦ Click **Add**.

The Dashboard launches, and your widget appears on the screen.

8 Click the **i** in the bottom-right corner of the widget.

The widget flips around to display custom edges and frames.

9 Click a new widget frame.

10 Click **Done** to finish the custom widget.

The widget flips around to display the new style.

● Optionally, you can click **Edit**, then click and drag in the frame or on the corners to adjust the widget, and then click **Done**.

Your new widget appears in the Dashboard.

Are there other ways to create custom widgets?

Yes. Leopard also includes an optional application called *Dashcode* for creating, testing, and editing widgets using a visual layout. Using Dashcode, you start by selecting a preset template or importing an existing widget. You can then drag in a link and customize the color and size of the widget. Dashcode includes a library of buttons that you can add to your widget design. You can go through a test run of your widget, and when it is ready, you can save it or even submit it to Apple.com so that others can download and use it.

Mac OS X Leopard not only makes everything you do with your computer easier, but it also protects your data from loss with an automatic backup system. The new Time Machine feature protects your data from accidental deletion or can help you restore your files in the event of a hard drive failure.

Backing Up

Copying your files and important data to a separate drive or another computer is the best way to protect them in case of theft, hardware failure or loss, or user errors such as accidental deletion. The difficult part has always been setting up a backup strategy and using it.

Automatic and Easy Backup

The Time Machine's simple-to-use and automatic setup makes backing up your data automatic. You select the location for the backup, what to include and exclude, and the time and frequency of the backup operation in System Preferences. The Time Machine acts in the background, making duplicates of your important data.

The First Backup

When you first install Leopard on a Mac, the installation asks if you want to use the Time Machine to back up your computer and guides you through the setup.

Incremental Changes

After it has made a complete backup of all the files on your system, including applications preferences, photos, and other documents, the Time Machine continues the process in the background backing up only the changes that you make.

Finding and Restoring

The Time Machine stores your data by date. You can select a date and look at your computer the way it was on that date and find an address or a complete folder of photos that you accidentally deleted. When you find the missing data, click it and click **Restore**, and the Time Machine replaces the data on your computer.

External Hard Drives

For the most protection and efficient backup, the Time Machine requires an external drive. You can purchase external hard drives with USB or FireWire connections in a variety of sizes. The more gigabytes, the more information can be stored and backed up.

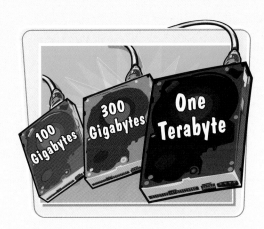

The Time Machine works automatically; however, by customizing the Time Machine Preferences, you can save space and back up precisely what you want and at the time of day that you select. You can also change where the backup is stored.

Customize Time Machine Backups

① Attach an external FireWire or USB hard drive.

② Click 🔘 in the Dock.

A dialog box appears.

③ Click **Set Up Time Machine**.

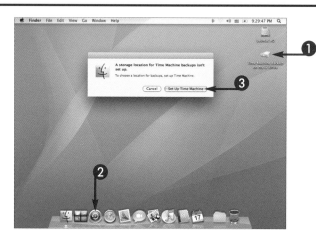

The Time Machine Preferences window opens.

④ Click **Configure**.

A dialog box appears.

5 Click to select the external drive for backing up.

● Optionally, you can click **Automatically delete backups older than** and click the ⬍ to select a timeframe for keeping backups.

6 Click **OK**.

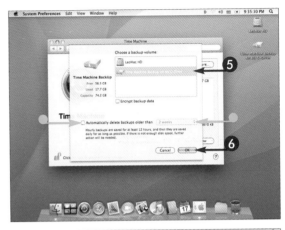

7 Click **Back up automatically** (☐ changes to ☑).

8 Click **Back Up Now**.

● Optionally, you can click ➕ to open a small dialog box. Click any items that you want to exclude from the backups and click **Exclude**.

The Time Machine Preferences window closes, and the backup begins.

Time Machine automatically backs up the drive or selected files every hour.

 TIPS

Why is the backup hard drive listed in the Do Not Back Up window?

The Time Machine is smart enough to recognize the backup drive and exclude it from backing it up to itself.

What is the difference between different types of external hard drives?

External hard drives have different gigabyte capacities and different types of connections, including USB and FireWire. Purchase an external hard drive that is substantially larger than your computer's hard drive so that you can save many versions of your data. You may want to have separate hard drives for backing up large numbers of photo or video files.

CHAPTER 12

Troubleshooting Mac Problems

Following simple maintenance as described in the previous chapter will help avoid many problematic situations. Although the Mac is among the most solid and reliable of computers, it is still a machine, and things can go wrong. The troubleshooting tasks in this chapter can help with many of the technical difficulties that can arise.

Quit Nonfunctioning Applications

Applications can stop functioning or freeze as you are working, and a spinning beach ball can sometimes appear and not stop. If you cannot quit a nonfunctioning application normally, you can force it to quit using the Apple menu, a keystroke, or the Dock, so you can continue with other applications without rebooting the computer.

DE-ICER
Force Quit
without
Rebooting
Your
Computer

Quit Nonfunctioning Applications

FORCE AN APPLICATION TO QUIT USING THE APPLE MENU

1 Click [apple].

2 Click **Force Quit**.

The Force Quit Applications dialog box appears.

3 Click the application to select it.

4 Click **Force Quit**.

The application quits.

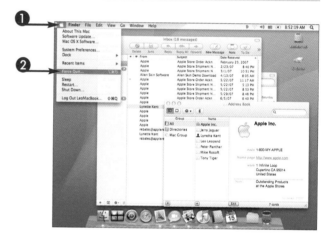

FORCE AN APPLICATION TO QUIT USING KEYSTROKES

1 Press ⌘ + Option + Esc.

The Force Quit Applications dialog box appears.

2 Perform the preceding steps **3** to **4** to force the application to quit.

FORCE AN APPLICATION TO QUIT USING THE DOCK

1 Press and hold Option.

2 Click and hold the application icon in the Dock.

3 Click **Force Quit**.

The application quits.

 TIPS

If I have to force an application to quit, what happens to my open documents?

Any unsaved changes in the open documents of a frozen application are lost when you force it to quit.

Can I reopen an application after forcing it to quit?

Yes. If the application freezes again, try restarting the computer and then launching it. If it still is not working, you may need to delete the application's Preferences file before launching it again or reinstall the application.

Delay an Update

If you are in the middle of a project and Software Update is about to install software requiring a restart, you can delay the install for a more-convenient time. If you have a fast Internet connection, you may want to download the updates but install them later when you may be using a slower connection or have no access to the Internet.

① Click .

② Click **Software Update**.

The Software Update window appears with a progress bar as it checks for new software.

Note: *You can also use the following steps if Software Update turns on automatically while you are working.*

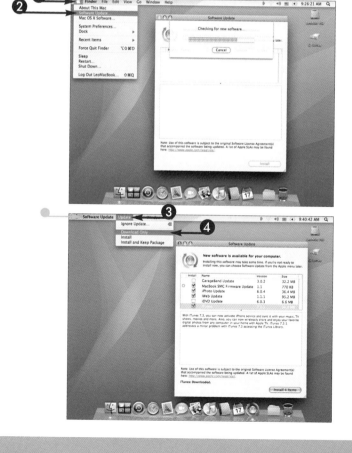

Note: indicates that a restart is required.

③ Click **Update**.

④ Click **Download Only**.

Software Update downloads the items to the Packages folder in the Library folder.

Note: *To install the updates, double-click your hard drive icon. Double-click the **Library** folder and then the **Packages** folder. Double-click any packages and follow the instructions.*

● Optionally, click **Software Update** and click **Quit Software Update** to run Software Update at a more convenient time.

Your Mac may have come with many preinstalled applications, or you may already have applications that you do not use. When you log in with the administrator user account, you can uninstall any application to free up disk space or to avoid conflicts if you have multiple versions of the same application installed.

Uninstall an Application

① Click [icon].

A Finder window appears.

② Click **Applications**.

③ Click and drag the application to be uninstalled to the Trash.

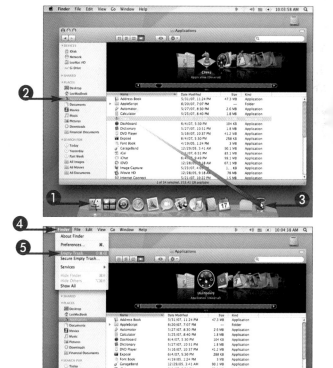

④ Click **Finder**.

⑤ Click **Empty Trash**.

The Finder empties the Trash and uninstalls the application.

Note: *Some third-party applications, such as Photoshop CS3, may include an uninstaller for removing the application.*

Delete
Locked Items

When you empty the Trash, you sometimes get a message that an item could not be deleted because it is locked. You can generally use a keystroke combination to empty the Trash. However, you may need to remove the item from the Trash to unlock it first.

Delete Locked Items

① Click **Finder**.

② Click **Empty Trash**.

A warning appears.

③ Click **OK**.

If an item in the Trash is locked, a message appears telling you so.

④ Click **Continue**.

The message disappears, and items other than the locked item are emptied from the Trash.

⑤ Press and hold Option .

⑥ Click **Finder**.

⑦ Click **Empty Trash**.

The Trash may empty the locked item.

8 If the locked item remains in the Trash, click .

The Trash folder opens.

9 Click the locked item to select it.

10 Press ⌘+I.

The Info window for that file or folder appears.

11 Click **Locked** (☑ changes to ☐).

12 Repeat steps **1** to **2**.

The Trash should empty.

Note: *If a folder for which you do not have write permission accidentally ends up in the Trash, you will not be able to empty that folder from the Trash.*

Are there any files that I should never put in the Trash?

You should not put the System Folder in the Trash or move items from the System Folder to the Trash. You should also be careful not to delete the Library folders. Another item that you should not move or delete is your Home folder. In general, most applications, including the iLife suite of applications and their respective media folders, should remain where they are automatically installed.

Fix Corrupt Preferences Files

Sometimes an application stops working properly. The Preferences file where an application saves information can become corrupt. You can often fix an errant application by deleting its Preferences file and restarting the application.

① Quit the errant application.

② Click [icon].

   A Finder window appears.

③ Click your Home folder.

④ Double-click **Library**.

The Library window appears.

⑤ Double-click **Preferences**.

320

The Preferences window appears.

6 Click and drag the errant application's Preferences file to the Trash.

7 Press ⌘ + Shift + Delete.

The Trash empties.

8 Relaunch the application.

● A new Preferences file appears in the Preferences window.

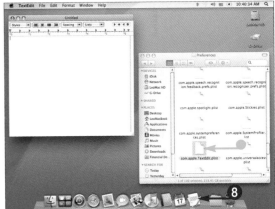

TIPS

How do I know which Preferences file to delete?

Application Preferences files usually follow a naming scheme **com.*vendor* .*applicationname*.plist.** For example, the Photo Booth Preferences file is named com.apple .PhotoBooth.plist.

Why is my Safari startup page different now that I deleted the Safari Preferences file?

Most applications rebuild a new Preferences file when the old one has been deleted. The new Preferences file includes the application's default settings, so you will have to reapply any special settings that you had changed.

Try a Different Startup Method

You must start up your computer from a different disk to install a new operating system or troubleshoot and repair your regular startup disk. You can start up from the operating system on a CD, DVD, or another internal drive. Depending on the model of your Macintosh, you can also start up using an external USB or FireWire drive that includes a startup operating system.

Try a Different Startup Method

START UP FROM A CD OR DVD

① Insert the CD or DVD with an operating system on it into your computer.

② Click 🍎.

③ Click **Restart**.

A warning asks if you are sure that you want to restart.

Note: *Pressing* Option *as you click* **Restart** *bypasses the warning dialog box and restarts the computer.*

④ Click **Restart**.

⑤ As the computer restarts, press and hold C.

Note: *Wait until the screen just goes dark before pressing and holding* C.

The computer restarts from the CD or DVD.

START UP FROM A DIFFERENT INTERNAL OR EXTERNAL HARD DRIVE

Note: *If starting from an external drive, connect it and turn it on.*

1 Click 📷.

2 Click **System Preferences**.

The System Preferences window appears.

3 Click **Startup Disk**.

A window appears with the available startup disks.

4 Click the new startup disk to select it.

5 Click **Restart**.

A warning message appears.

6 Click **Restart** in the message dialog box.

The computer restarts from the new startup disk.

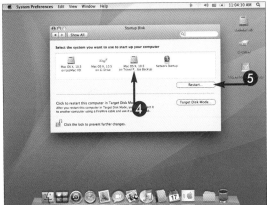

TIP

Are there other ways to restart from a separate drive?

On most computers, you can press and hold Option after you click **Restart**. The computer begins the startup process by displaying all the available startup drives. This can take several seconds. Use the mouse to click the startup drive that you want to use and press Return. You can also connect two computers using a FireWire cable and start up a computer in Target disk mode. See Chapter 7 for details on starting up and using Target disk mode.

Erase Discs with Disk Utility

The Disk Utility application included with Mac OS X Leopard enables you to control numerous maintenance tasks. You can use Disk Utility to erase CD-RW and DVD-RW media so that you can record new items to these rewritable discs. You can also use Disk Utility to erase external hard drives and prepare them to install a system or for recording files.

Erase Discs with Disk Utility

Note: *You must have a SuperDrive or one capable of writing to DVD media to use DVD-R/RW or DVD+R/RW discs.*

① Click .

A Finder window opens.

② Click **Applications**.

③ Press Option and double-click **Utilities**.

The Utilities folder opens, and the Applications window closes.

④ Press Option and double-click **Disk Utility**.

The Disk Utility application launches, and the Utilities window closes.

5 Click the CD-R or DVD-R drive in the left section of the window.

The window options change.

6 Insert a CD-RW or DVD-RW disc into the CD/DVD drive.

Note: *Depending what is on the CD-RW or DVD-RW, a dialog box may appear. Click **Ignore** if you plan to erase the disc or make another selection.*

7 Click **Completely** (○ changes to ◉).

8 Click **Erase**.

Note: *It can take a long time to erase the disc.*

 TIPS

There are several hard drive icons that appear when I attach my external hard drive. Which one do I select?

An external drive appears along with all its volumes in the left side of the window. Clicking the drive and clicking **Erase** erases all the data on the drive, including any separate volumes, and leaves the disk empty. Clicking a volume below the drive and clicking **Erase** erases only that volume and leaves the rest of the drive intact.

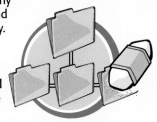

Should I select the Erase Free Space option for erasing an external hard drive?

Clicking **Erase Free Space** offers three different methods of erasing your files so that they cannot be recovered. You should use one of these methods to securely erase all data and make it unrecoverable before giving the hard drive to someone else for their use.

Repair Disk Permissions

Because Mac OS X is a multiuser environment, each file on the hard drive has permissions describing who can access files or open applications. If the computer runs slowly or documents do not open correctly, the permissions may be altered. You can repair disk permissions using Disk Utility and should generally repair them after any software installation.

Repair Disk Permissions

1 Press ⌘ + **Shift** + **U**.

The Utilities folder appears.

2 Press **Option** and double-click **Disk Utility**.

The Disk Utility application launches, and the Utilities window closes.

3 Click the disk in the left section of the window.

4 Click **First Aid**.

5 Click **Repair Disk Permissions**.

Disk Utility tests and repairs the disk permissions.

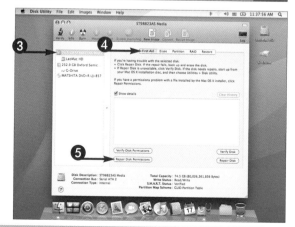

You can sometimes repair a malfunctioning drive with the Disk Utility application. To repair the startup disk, you must restart from another disk with an operating system as shown earlier in this chapter in the section "Try a Different Startup Method." To repair a disk drive other than the startup disk, you must close all files and quit any running applications on the disk to be repaired.

Repair a Disk

1 Press ⌘ + Shift + U.

The Utilities folder appears.

2 Press Option and double-click **Disk Utility**.

The Disk Utility application launches, and the Utilities window closes.

3 Click the disk to be repaired in the left section of the window.

Note: Repair Disk will be grayed out for the startup disk in use.

4 Click **First Aid**.

5 Click **Repair Disk**.

Disk Utility tests and repairs the disk if possible.

Using Third-Party Utilities

Your Mac comes with the Apple Hardware Test application on a disc, and purchasing the AppleCare protection plan includes the TechTool Deluxe utility CD. Although you can start up from these discs and run the tests to check for any hardware defects, third parties make more encompassing hardware- and software-testing utilities that can check as well as repair many hardware and software problems.

Disk Directory Problems

The disk directory is the map that the computer uses to find items. If the directory is corrupted, the computer cannot function properly. Alsoft's DiskWarrior is one of the most-powerful disk directory repair programs available and can replace a defective directory and recover lost files and folders.

Hardware and Software Problems

Because problems can arise from a variety of causes, Micromat's TechTool Pro runs a series of tests to diagnose and repair hardware components, recover directories and data, and more. The complete version of TechTool Pro includes individual repair tools and repair suites that run automatically.

TechTool's Protégé and DiskWarrior CD

Using both TechTool Pro and DiskWarrior on startup CDs or DVDs is an excellent solution. TechTool's Protégé is a bootable 1GB FireWire drive with TechTool and other utilities preloaded. You can install DiskWarrior on the Protégé for the ultimate repair tool.

General Precautions

Before running any utility, you should back up your data to a separate disc or drive. Cleaning up the hard drive by deleting unnecessary files and folders and emptying the Trash can also help the utilities function better.

What Causes Disk Problems?

Disk errors happen for many reasons. Computer hardware can malfunction. Added RAM can be incompletely seated in the retaining clips or may be incompatible with the computer. A very full hard drive with no room to process files or a software application bug can corrupt files. Shutting down the computer using the power switch can corrupt the directory. Unplugging external drives without properly removing them first can corrupt data. Power surges and power failures interrupt file access and damage hardware, causing many disk errors.

Index

Index

Index

Index